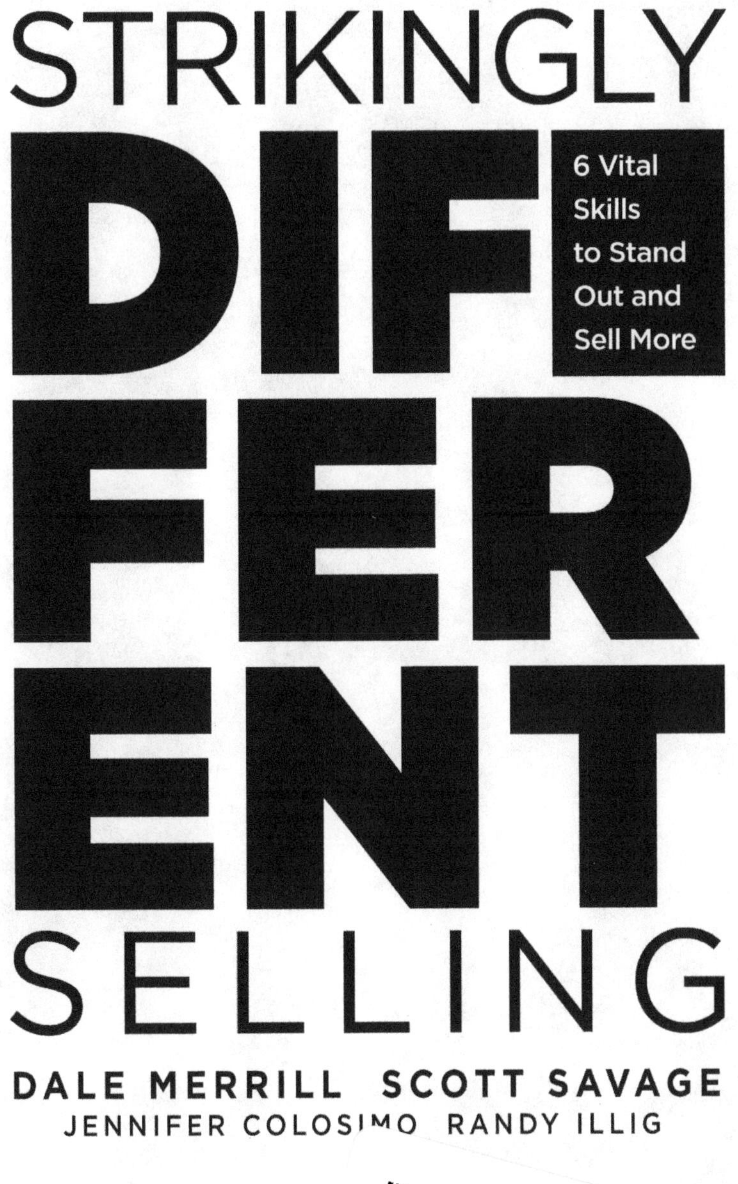
STRIKINGLY
DIFFERENT
6 Vital Skills to Stand Out and Sell More
SELLING
DALE MERRILL SCOTT SAVAGE
JENNIFER COLOSIMO RANDY ILLIG

D0488723

STRIKINGLY DIFFERENT SELLING

6 Vital Skills to Stand Out and Sell More

DALE MERRILL SCOTT SAVAGE
JENNIFER COLOSIMO RANDY ILLIG

The Sales Performance Experts at FranklinCovey

CORAL GABLES

Published by Mango Publishing, a division of Mango Publishing Group, Inc.

Cover Design: Roberto Nuñez
Layout & Design: The FranklinCovey Creative Lab

For permission requests, please contact the publisher at:
Mango Publishing Group
2850 S Douglas Road, 4th Floor
Coral Gables, FL 33134 USA
info@mango.bz

For special orders, quantity sales, course adoptions, and corporate sales, please email the publisher at sales@mango.bz. For trade and wholesale sales, please contact Ingram Publisher Services at customer.service@ingramcontent.com or +1.800.509.4887.

Strikingly Different Selling: 6 Vital Skills to Stand Out and Sell More

Library of Congress Cataloging-in-Publication number: 2021946731
ISBN: (print) 978-1-64250-486-6, (ebook) 978-1-64250-487-3
BISAC category code BUS058000, BUSINESS & ECONOMICS / Sales & Selling / General

Printed in the United States of America

TABLE OF CONTENTS

BECOME STRIKINGLY DIFFERENT ONLINE AND IN PERSON

Mark was facing a daunting challenge. As a managing director at a global professional services company, he was proposing on a huge technology outsourcing deal. The client viewed the requested services as a commodity (i.e., anyone could provide them), the competitors were three strong companies that competed solely on price, and Mark's company was at the higher end of price and value. He needed a way to stand out and create contrast between his company and the competition or he would have no chance to win. We met Mark in Bangalore, India two months before the proposal was due and coached him on the formula and skills of Strikingly Different Selling. Mark embraced everything we shared and completely changed his approach to the pursuit.

Two months later, Mark and his team were awarded a $16-million contract, along with praise from the client that his team's proposal stood out as crisp, different, and compelling.

After the win, Mark told us that to stand out, he looked at everything his team was planning to say and do in the proposal through the lens of Strikingly Different Selling: Is this **relevant** (focusing on what matters most to the client), **distinct** (showing something different and better than the competition or status quo), and **memorable** (easy to share and hard to forget)? And, according to Mark, the formula and skills made all the difference in the win.

This book is about how to stand out and sell more. It's about becoming Strikingly *Different.* When something is Strikingly *Different,* it is clearly different and better than its comparison.

The overwhelming evidence shows that the inability of salespeople to stand out is a pervasive issue with costly consequences. Working with sales research firm Primary Intelligence, we analyzed the results of surveys with more than 5,000 business-to-business (B2B) decision makers on deals. We found that average win rates were a dismal 17 percent for deals above $100,000 across multiple industries globally.[1] What's going wrong?

Until now, there have been lots of questions and rarely any helpful answers. Certainly, the sales environment has only intensified in the past decade. COVID-19 massively accelerated the tectonic shift from live to virtual (i.e., live-online) selling. A recent Bain survey found that 80 percent of buyers and sellers believe there will be a sustained increase in virtual interactions.[2] In other words, virtual selling is here to stay. In the live-online world, the classic techniques of selling are much less effective, sales pipelines are languishing, and the look and feel of buyer-seller interactions is very different. It's harder and harder for buyers to tell the difference between one salesperson's offerings and another's. Everyone looks and sounds the same. Competition is intense. As a result, many salespeople are having a hard time getting first meetings, are conducting plenty of additional meetings that go nowhere, and are simply not winning enough business.

HOW CAN SELLERS STAND OUT?

The primary question today is: **How can sellers stand out as different and better when the competition is at such a high level?**

While the challenges of standing out are intensified in the live-online world, they are similar to the challenges of standing out in person. And the four of us authors know firsthand how difficult it is to stand out.

1 Allred, Ken (2021). Buyers' Perceptions of Differentiation in B2B Purchase Decisions—Primary Intelligence Report, March 5, 2021, 9.

2 Bain & Company (2021). Fact or Fiction? The four myths of B2B selling. Retrieved May 28, 2021, from https://www.bain.com/contentassets/5ea802ac361f4e39b372313a9303e4f4/virtualb2bselling2.pdf

We've tried, failed, and succeeded in numerous settings. Each of us has personally hit and missed sales targets, mastered the online sales environment, and led teams in the pursuit of greatness.

As sales thought leaders and practitioners at the global performance improvement company FranklinCovey, we advise salespeople representing many of the top technology, consulting, and professional services organizations across the globe. In the course of our work, we discovered three frustrating struggles most salespeople seem to have in common when it comes to standing out:

1. How can I come up with differentiated messages for my clients?
2. How do I pull the messages together into a cohesive set of stories?
3. How will I share these stories with clients in a compelling way?

Through deal advancement work sessions, opportunity reviews, and other sales activities, we've helped thousands of salespeople overcome these struggles and gain confidence in their ability to craft, shape, and deliver compelling messages that enable them to stand out from the start to the finish of their sales cycles.

In addition to our frontline experience and ongoing advisory work, we had a unique opportunity to get feedback from client executives on what matters most to them when talking with salespeople. This came about when several global companies engaged us to participate in live sales simulations over a period of six years. As part of these engagements, we saw both sides of nearly 1,700 sales interactions where we had front-row seats as silent observers. This was fascinating work because we watched more than 2,800 experienced salespeople in sales meetings with senior client executives all along the sales cycle. We attended the meetings as observers, then interviewed the salespeople and client executives afterwards. It was an incredible opportunity to speak candidly to the selling teams and the clients.

The salespeople we observed were highly paid and talented professionals. They were exceptionally educated and had long résumés. We expected greatness, solid selling fundamentals, market-leading expertise, and remarkable people skills. And as we interviewed the salespeople after each interaction, we heard the following common responses:

- "I think the meeting went well. It wasn't perfect, but we felt there was good interaction, and we definitely got what we needed."
- "That was a solid meeting. I think we did a good job asking questions and exploring their business challenges. The client executive seems to like us and clearly wants to engage in further discussions."
- "They love our solution, our implementation plan, and how clearly different we are from our competitors. We are in a great position to win this opportunity!"

But then we spoke with the client executives.

Well over 70 percent of the time, the response from the client executive was some version of this: *"That meeting was a waste of my time, and in a real pursuit, they would not be invited back."*

How was it possible that all these talented salespeople could be so far off the mark? How could so many of them think they were doing a great job, while disappointing the client over and over again?

What was more intriguing is that after observing nearly 1,700 interactions, it became clear that we were not witnessing an odd occurrence in a sales simulation. Rather, we were witnessing the reality of what most clients are experiencing every day when meeting online or in person with salespeople: lackluster interactions and disappointing results.

SURPRISINGLY AVERAGE TO STRIKINGLY DIFFERENT

As we debriefed the meetings with client executives, a surprising theme emerged: clients entered every sales meeting hoping against hope to see something distinct and relevant, whether in the message, the thought leadership, the way the salesperson asked questions, the dialogue, or the solutions. But the vast majority of the salespeople they encountered were simply indistinguishable.

This phenomenon was validated in additional research with Primary Intelligence, where we analyzed the results of surveys with more than 14,500 B2B decision makers. Buyers saw no difference between vendors 42 percent of the time. We began calling this phenomenon the *Surprisingly Average.*

Consider that as sales professionals, regardless of the industry, we're working with similar technology, approaches, people, and methodologies. In fact, most of us are solving similar problems with similarly long lists of client references and claims on the same outcomes. Again, we appear to be remarkably similar, therefore Surprisingly Average.

But clients make decisions based on *differences*, not similarities. By the nature of the sales process, the client will expect some common ground between vendors, and we do often have to check off certain criteria, perhaps in our response to a request for proposal (RFP). But in the final analysis, the differences between options make the biggest impact when it comes to decision making, where it's not good enough just to be different. The salesperson must demonstrate differences that *matter to the client.*

Appearing in contrast to their competitors isn't news to sales professionals. They know they need to create this contrast, but they struggle to define "contrast" in a way that helps clients *act* on it. Because the client executives in our simulations had a vested interest in helping the salespeople get better, we were able to work with them to investigate what did and didn't work, and the reasons why. We spent hundreds of hours with the client executives discussing, debating, testing, and learning together how salespeople could become Strikingly Different.

Through our research and client work, we hit upon the simple formula for achieving compelling contrast that our client Mark and thousands of salespeople are successfully using to stand out:

RELEVANT + DISTINCT + MEMORABLE (RDM) = STRIKINGLY DIFFERENT

Relevant: Focus on what matters most to the client.

Distinct: Show something that is different and better.

Memorable: Make it "sticky": easy to share and hard to forget.

Seeing the world through the RDM lens will change how you see yourself, your clients, and every sales opportunity. RDM is brought to life in the six skills described below.

The first four skills will help you **CONNECT and ENGAGE** with your clients by exploring provocative ideas, experience, and future possibilities. The goal is to build a Strikingly Different message house that contains all your client messages under one roof. The foundation of the house is RDM, the roof is your main message, and the structural beams in between are your key supporting messages.

Strikingly Different Message House

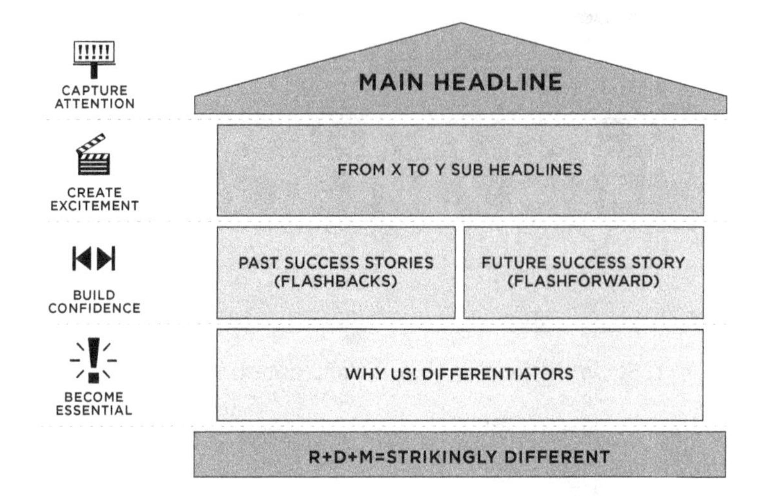

- **Skill 1** is about how to **capture the client's attention** with a verbal billboard in any setting at any time. It is your core message for the client.
- **Skill 2** is about how to **create excitement** with brief verbal or written movie trailers to get meetings, start meetings or proposals, and end meetings with increasing momentum.
- **Skill 3** is about how to **build confidence** with flashbacks (i.e., success stories) where you've helped other clients, and a flashforward where you help your current client see a clear path to go from where they are now to a different and better future.
- **Skill 4** is about how to **become essential** with Why Us! differentiators. Here you highlight unique differences and help the client see why those differences matter.

The last two skills do not appear in the message house. These skills will help you partner with your client to **VALIDATE and CO-CREATE** the messages of the house so it eventually looks like, feels like, and becomes *their* house. When that happens, you and the client win together.

- **Skill 5** is about how to get curious and find the gaps in the message house.
- **Skill 6** is about how to navigate traffic lights, close the gaps, and complete the house.

We'll show you how all six skills come together through a sample middle-stage discussion in the chapter titled "Pulling It All Together." You'll notice that throughout this book, we discuss how to apply these skills in online sales interactions, but if you'd like more details, we've included an appendix at the end of this book on how to conduct winning sales interactions online and through video conferencing platforms.

Whether you've just started on your sales career or you're at the top of your game, we're confident the formula and skills in this book will help you dramatically change your client interactions and results online and in person. They will help you go *from* just one in the crowd *to* consistently standing out as the different and better choice. We invite you to dive in, give it your best, and work hard to become Strikingly Different. It will be well worth your time.

PART 1
CONNECT & ENGAGE

Skill 1:
CAPTURE ATTENTION WITH VERBAL BILLBOARDS

Strikingly Different Message House

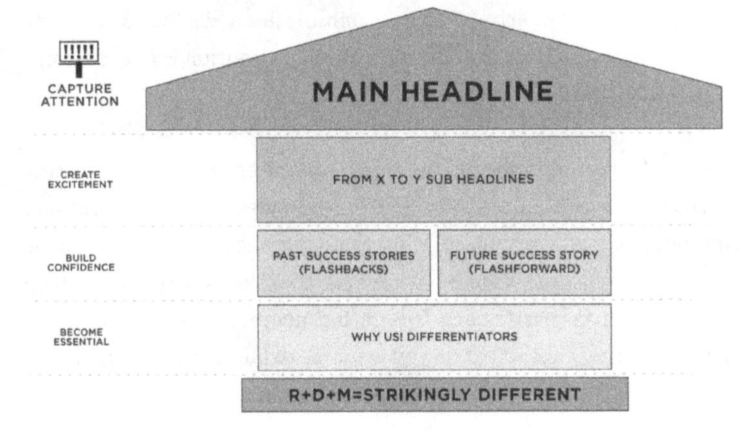

Recall our Asia Pacific-based client Mark in the introduction, who used the Strikingly Different RDM formula and skills to win a $16 million contract. In the first step of that process, Mark and his team captured the client's attention quickly and kept it with the following "billboard" (shared verbally and in writing) that had key messages in client-relevant language.

Empower <CLIENT> IT as an indispensable, leading-edge strategic partner to the business

- ✔ **Improve business process compliance massively** *from* present levels *to* >98% from Day Zero, thereby **maximizing** the **business case benefits.**
- ✔ **Accelerate** <CLIENT> *from* the current state *to* a new **technology-enabled** proactive **growth engine** within the first 12 months.
- ✔ **Move** *from* a manual, high incident-volume support service *to* a **proactive, hyper-automated service** from Day Zero where *"The best ticket in the world is the one that does not exist."*

Mark's Final Billboard

After observing nearly 1,700 sales simulations, we found, as Mark did, the best way to grab and keep a client's attention is to use a well-crafted billboard.

The billboard metaphor came from a client executive after sitting through a series of sales meetings where the salespeople droned on and on about themselves, their solution, their approach, and never got to the point. Their messages were not concise, not clear, and not focused on the client. In one particularly frustrating meeting, the client said, "OK, let's get to the point. What do you want me to know? Sum it up. Give it to me in a billboard." We loved the idea and ran with it.

What's fun about real billboards is their whole purpose is to grab your attention for a split second and compel you to remember something valuable about the product. The advertising industry has mastered communicating value quickly. After all, when you only have a split second of someone's attention, your message has to be simple and straightforward.

We were convinced that salespeople could learn a lot from billboards about concision and delivering an enticing message in seconds. We began testing various forms of sales billboards in the simulations and with numerous clients in the field for several years until we came up with the simple pattern described below that is now used by thousands of successful salespeople around the world.

CAPTURE ATTENTION WITH SALES BILLBOARDS

In a sales context, a **billboard** is your core message for the client. It consists of a highly captivating main headline and three sub headlines that entice your client to keep listening. The themes carry through to all the other messages in the Strikingly Different message house.

Can a few headlines really do that much? Absolutely—in fact, they have to. When your clients have decisions to make, challenges to overcome, and business strategies to execute, they don't want to be bogged down and held up. With planning and preparation, you can offer something to the client that has enough merit to stop them and entice them to listen. Once they have listened, they may want to share their perspective, and if that goes well, they may want to have a dialogue. There is plenty of time for sincere and active listening once the client is engaged and the discussion moves forward. But only if your first few words hit the mark. Let us be clear on this point: Clients do not want the precious first minutes of a meeting to be a fishing expedition. If you asked for the meeting, go in with something prepared and intriguing for the client to consider, and present it quickly. (The time for exploration and validation is later in the conversation. We'll show you an effective way to do this in Skill 5.)

TWO REASONS SALES BILLBOARDS WORK

1. **Billboards are concise.** Humans have short attention spans—as brief as eight seconds, according to a Microsoft study.[3] Billboards communicate an intriguing client-focused message in just a few seconds.
2. **Billboards are focused on client outcomes, not salesperson solutions.** Clients want to see and hear a message that is crisp, sharp, and focused on them. They don't want a rambling message focused on a salesperson's company or solution.

FOLLOW THE PATTERN OF AN EFFECTIVE SALES BILLBOARD

1. Think and speak in headlines.
2. Link to the client's goals and issues.
3. Show From–To client outcomes.

Thinking and speaking in headlines will help you be concise. **Linking** to the client's goals and issues will help you be relevant, focusing on what matters most to the client. **Showing** From–To client outcomes will help you be distinct by contrasting where the client is today with where the client could be tomorrow. We recommend using From–To statements as often as possible to bring contrast to our ideas (and ourselves as sellers). There is another compelling benefit of showing From–To client outcomes. The human mind creates drama and intrigue more powerfully than anything we could say. When we associate From–To outcomes with related symptoms and emotions, clients paint a vivid image in their mind of the current state contrasted with the promised future state, depending on the effectiveness of our words. They *feel* something rather than just understand what we are saying. And, in the process, the client's motivation to explore possibilities with us increases significantly.

---

3 McSpadden, Kevin. "You now have a shorter attention span than a goldfish." *Time*, May 14, 2015. https://time.com/3858309/attention-spans-goldfish/

What a Sales Billboard Is Not

A sales billboard is not a lengthy, rambling list of facts, data, and bullet points focused on you, your organization, and your solutions. You've heard the phrase "a picture is worth a thousand words." And many salespeople have the picture—a slide deck and beautiful sales materials—but then they still share the thousand words as well. We have to stop this habit; it's painful for our clients. Billboards help us avoid this trap.

A Verbal Billboard is **Not:**

A lengthy, rambling list of facts, data, and bullet points focused on you, your company, and your solutions!

Creating Effective Headlines

Headlines are the heart of a great sales billboard. Here are several real-world examples contrasting *Surprisingly Average* with *Strikingly Different* headlines from some of our clients.

COMPANY	SURPRISINGLY AVERAGE HEADLINE	STRIKINGLY DIFFERENT HEADLINE
Customer Relationship Management Platform Company	Make resource decisions faster.	Cut the time to make resource decisions from >4 weeks to <2 hours.
Data Center Company	Provision dedicated connectivity and hyperconverged infrastructure faster.	Deploy new infrastructure in hours/days, not weeks/months.
Truck Driver Recruiting Company	We have flexible driving schedules.	From unpredictable schedules to being home when you want to be.
Professional Services Company	Streamline your maintenance ticket process.	Go from SOLVING maintenance tickets to AVOIDING tickets.
Healthcare Services Provider	We will improve your members' health outcomes.	You will lower costs by up to 11% *and* realize better health outcomes at the same time.
Farming Cooperative	Close the books much faster than you're already doing.	Go from the stress and frustration of closing the books in six weeks to the relief and satisfaction of closing them in five days.

Look at the last headline in the table above. Notice the contrast between the Surprisingly Average headline on the left, *"Close the books much faster than you're already doing,"* and the outcomes, symptoms, and emotions in the Strikingly Different headline on the right, *"Go from the stress and frustration of closing the books in six weeks to the relief and satisfaction of closing them in five days."* How would you come up with those words? Imagine that through either early conversation with the client or a judicious assumption, you know the company's executives are demanding the numbers as close to period end as possible. Bankers need the numbers sooner to satisfy loan covenants. Salespeople's commissions are late when the sales numbers aren't validated until the books are closed. Everyone is demanding the financial team get the books closed faster with no errors, but the current disconnected systems and processes make that impossible. What would the financial team likely be feeling? Probably stressed, pressured, overwhelmed, frustrated, and resentful. How would they feel if they could close the books in just five days? Likely relieved, valued, and satisfied. Using the client's description of symptoms and/or emotions, coupled with the dramatic outcome of moving from six weeks to five days to close the books, transforms the headline from boring into something that stands out and causes the client to feel something and then do something.

HOW TO BUILD A COMPELLING SALES BILLBOARD

Follow this writing process to quickly create a compelling sales billboard that contains your core message for the client.

1. Start by capturing key themes about the current state and desired future state of the client.
2. Boil your key themes down and turn them into three compelling From–To sub headlines.
3. Now, step back and look at all three From–To sub headlines and write a persuasive one-sentence From–To main headline that captures the big idea for your client. Make sure it will create intrigue and cause someone to want to listen to the rest of your message.

Don't worry about being too clever when crafting your billboard. Be honest and reflect the essence and motivating idea of your story. But watch out: After helping hundreds of salespeople create compelling billboards, we've learned that salespeople can almost always create their From–To sub headlines faster and easier than they can figure out their main headline. So, it's usually not a good idea to try to come up with your main headline before you've created three sub headlines. Expect it to be an iterative process where you start with key themes, craft sub headlines, *then* write your main headline.

Billboard Builder Example

Let's walk through a real-life example of how to follow the process to build a great sales billboard. We recently met Matthew in a live-online *Strikingly Different* work session we ran for his employer, a leading consulting company. Matthew was an executive who specialized in marketing operations. He needed to build a sales billboard to use with a marketing executive at Walmart. Here is the process he followed from start to finish. With some coaching from us, this took Matthew about twenty to thirty minutes.

We noticed Matthew was listening intently as we described the concepts around developing great billboards and shared several real-life examples. We asked him and his colleagues to work individually and then we put them into groups of three in Zoom breakout rooms.

Key Themes (first edition)

The left-hand column shows current state—what they need to move FROM. The right-hand column shows future state—what they could move TO.

FROM		TO
1. Two different customer experiences going on in-store and online.	▶	1. Give customers a single experience whether they shop online or in-store.
2. Walmart's share of customers' wallet is decreasing due to intense competition from Amazon and other retailers.		2. Increase Walmart's share of customers' wallet by improving customer experience.
3. Lots of unsold goods left on the shelves and online because customers aren't getting the products they want.		3. Use targeted marketing to reduce unsold goods and get customers the right products at the right prices.
4. Marketing is viewed as just another business function.		4. Turn marketing into a strategic value generator.

We joined Matthew's breakout room and asked him to share his draft billboard with us. His themes were strong. We coached him to use fewer words and to come up with stronger From–To sub headlines that illustrated the contrast between Walmart's current state and desired future state. It took him three iterations to go from average, to good, to great.

Sub Headlines (second edition)

This is the boiled down version of the current state and future state themes, written as compelling **From—To** sub headlines.

1. Move FROM an "in-store" OR "online" experience TO a single customer experience and increase share of wallet by 10%.

2. Reduce unsold goods by 9% using targeted marketing campaigns to get customers the products they want at the prices they need.

3. Transform marketing FROM just another business function TO a strategic value generator.

As shown above, Matthew's third iteration of sub headlines was compelling.

Matthew's initial main headline was *"Change your customer mindset FROM 'I only go to Walmart for a few things' TO 'I go to Walmart for everything.'"* That was a good headline but likely not provocative enough to capture the Walmart executive's attention. After a bit of coaching to push the envelope, Matt created his final main headline, *"Change your customer mindset FROM 'I'll just get it from Amazon' TO 'I go to Walmart for everything.'"* That headline is Strikingly Different and grabs your attention.

Main Headline (final edition)

This is the **From—To** MAIN HEADLINE that captures the BIG idea. This should create intrigue and cause someone to want to listen to the rest of your message.

Change your customer mindset FROM "I'll just get it from Amazon" TO "I go to Walmart for everything."

Matthew's billboard was his core message for the Walmart marketing executive. It was the roof of his Strikingly Different message house.

WHERE DO YOU GET INFORMATION FOR BILLBOARDS?

With a new client, and sometimes even with existing clients, we may not be initially aware of their specific goals or issues, so how do we draft a billboard in that case? It may take some dialogue; guesses based on their website, earnings calls, press releases, social media; or experiences that we've had in the industry or with other clients. Doing enough research to be relevant and distinct is vital when building your billboard.

Push yourself to include outcomes whenever possible. For example, let's say you were creating billboard sub headlines for a healthcare system executive you want to meet with. Based on outcomes you've helped other healthcare systems achieve, you might feel confident writing this headline: *"Improve patient satisfaction from the twenty-sixth to the seventy-fifth percentile within twelve months,"* calibrating to be more conservative if you need to. And note that we specifically said, "within twelve months." Including a timeframe is a small change that can often make the From–To statements more insightful and likely to spark a conversation about your experience.

During a meeting with the client, these From–To statements will be up for debate...and they should be! Clients generally love to engage with these statements. When you're in early stages, remember that these statements aren't commitments or a proposal. They communicate that you want to discuss these ideas so you can understand more about what's happening for the client and become more relevant to their situation.

Remember: think and speak in headlines, trying to make them as relevant to the client's goals and issues as possible. Each client, and industry, requires a different look and feel, and we always want you to create your billboards in your personal style. If some of the examples here don't sound like something you would say, change them!

Essentially, you are taking a hypothesis from your past experience or what you're seeing in the market, then having a dialogue with the client so you can wrestle through what's relevant for them, what sticks, and what seems distinct. You start with a hypothesis and then co-develop it as you move forward.

You can use a billboard via an email (putting your main headline in the subject line), the first few minutes of a phone call or live-online meeting, a social media request, when you bump into someone in the hallway, at a social event, or to start a meeting.

And billboards aren't just for first meetings or initial contacts. You will refine your billboard throughout the sales cycle, validating and co-creating with key client stakeholders. Your billboard, including your main headline and From–To sub headlines can, and should, evolve over time as you learn more about how to make them increasingly relevant to the client. Ultimately, your main headline should turn into the client's win theme, supported with compelling From–To sub headlines.

By the final presentation, you should have a very sharp, validated billboard to open the meeting, one that has been tested and vetted by the client themselves.

Recently, we were helping some top salespeople at a technology company come up with the main headline to use with one of their customers. Within a short time, they knew the headline was working when the CEO of that company used their headline "All on one device" to describe the company's future at a meeting with stock analysts. In this case, the salesperson's vision of how they could help became the *customer's* headline of how they were going to win in the market. That's the ultimate goal of a billboard.

BEST PRACTICES FOR USING BILLBOARDS

- **Adjust your billboard for each stakeholder.** Your billboard will change a little or a lot depending on who you're talking to.

Some of the themes may stay the same, and you will likely tweak a From–To statement as you move through the organization to different lines of business. Make sure your main headline captures the big idea that's going to be the most powerful for that particular individual, supported with up to three From–To sub headlines.

- **Have a few billboards in your back pocket.** Although you will likely create custom billboards for each client, we also recommend having a couple of billboards ready to use that generally apply to your most common client/industry scenarios.
- **Creating billboards is a skill you can learn and practice.** None of us are advertising execs, but salespeople can become quite skilled at creating these billboards. As you continue to work at this, you'll get better and better. Think and speak in headlines in as many client interactions as possible. The more you write them, the better you will get at expressing just the right balance of outcomes, symptoms, and emotions that will resonate with a particular client. Seek feedback from colleagues who understand the pattern for effective sales billboards. Be willing to accept hard-to-hear feedback and apply it to your billboard. Often when we work with clients, they start out with a wordy value message that lacks an effective From–To statement (e.g., our experience with Matthew described earlier in this chapter), but that's expected! Usually, if we listen for a few minutes and help them refine it, they get pretty good by the second or third try. By the fourth or fifth, it's usually strong enough for us to think, *Yes, we'd be willing to engage with you to explore that further.* So don't stop on your first try—iterate through at least three versions for the best results. Don't let the learning curve frustrate you. It's not just a skill you read about and then it magically works. But if you keep at it, you'll find yourself getting better and better.

Real-Life Billboard Scenarios

In addition to Mark and Matthew's billboards, let's look at a few more examples of real-life billboards based on experiences with our clients. We'll ask you to draft your response, then we'll share the billboard that succeeded in real life.

In the first scenario, imagine you're meeting with a digital services executive at a global media company dealing with three digital challenges: deploying apps is taking too long, backing up and moving data to different clouds and back to on-premises is difficult and prone to errors, and data analytics are slow. The client expressed a lot of frustration with their current situation. You know from your experience with other clients that your solutions made their cloud back-ups 90 percent faster and improved the speed of their data analytics speed by thirty times.

What would a billboard look like?

Your response: ______________________________

____

____

____

____

____

____

Our suggestion:

Verbal Billboard Example: Global Media Giant
Go from Slow Moving to Digital Speed

1. **Test and Deploy** apps in hours/days, not weeks/months.
2. **Backup/Restore** to cloud 90% faster than today.
3. **Automate** data analytics 30x faster than your competitors.

Now let's say you're meeting with the senior director of Information Technology at a large consumer packaged goods company (they make tasty snacks). They are looking to improve their efficiency and margins by making IT more relevant to the business, outsourcing most of their IT operating functions, and moving *all* their applications to the cloud.

What would a billboard look like?

Your response: ____

____

____

____

____

____

____

____

Our suggestion:

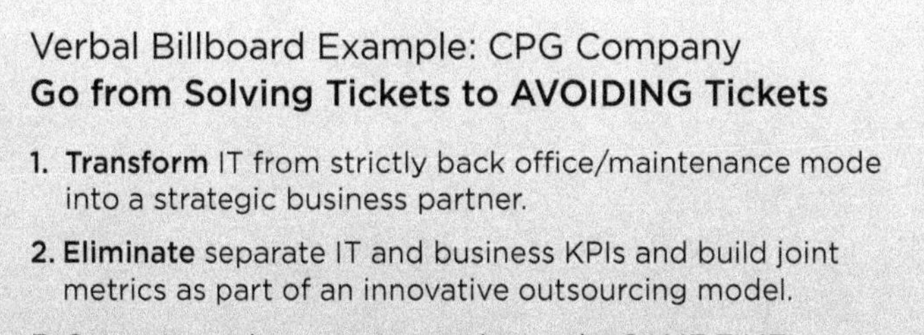

Exercise: Practice Building Your Billboards

Using the examples above, try creating a billboard and share it with a colleague. Have your partner give you feedback on how the billboard grabs them (or not). Is it relevant, distinct, and memorable? Remember, you don't need the main headline and sub headlines to be too cute or slick. What grab most clients, most of the time, are From–To statements that directly address their key issues, challenges, or drivers of what's happening today in their business.

Make sure to keep the headlines as relevant to their specific organization as possible with the words, the emotion, and the symptoms. The more relevant to their situation, the more likely the message will resonate with them.

Once we've successfully captured our client's attention with a billboard, we need to act fast to grow that spark into full-blown excitement. We'll do that in the next chapter by adding nuance, color, and context to the billboard in an expanded version we call a "movie trailer."

KEY INSIGHTS FOR SKILL 1

- Use billboards to capture attention and keep it through the sales cycle.
- Follow the pattern of an effective sales billboard:

  1. Think and speak in headlines.
  2. Link to the client's goals and issues.
  3. Show From–To client outcomes.

- Evaluate your billboard through the lens of the Strikingly Different formula:

Relevant

- Are your headlines focused on what matters most to the client and not on what you want to sell?

Distinct

- Is the **To** clearly better than the **From** while also creating intrigue in your main headline and each of your sub headlines?
- Does your billboard tell an easy-to-follow story?
- Is it compelling?

Memorable

- Is your billboard easy to share and hard to forget?

Skill 2:
CREATE EXCITEMENT WITH MOVIE TRAILERS

Strikingly Different Message House

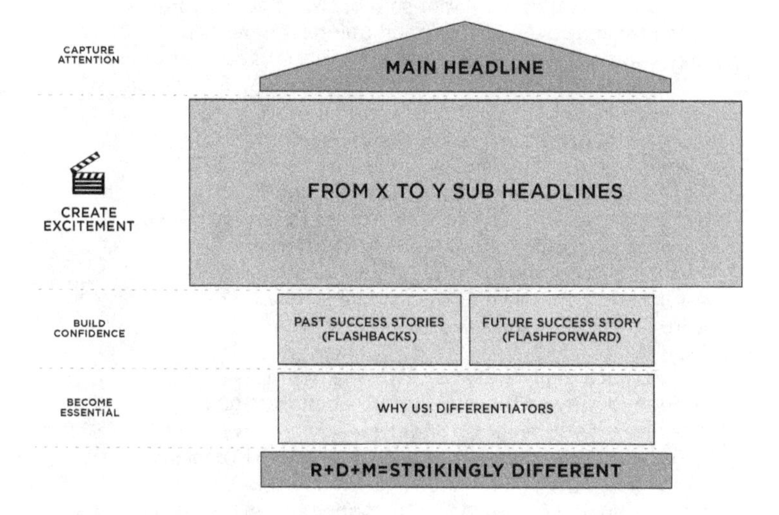

After years of successful selling at Xerox, our colleague and friend Julie Schmidt decided to jump into a new industry. Like most seasoned sales professionals changing companies, she had high expectations and was excited to build a book of business. However, when confronted with a completely new selling environment, no existing clients, and the necessity of building a robust pipeline, she began to find this environment more challenging than expected.

She told us, "I needed to get more people to talk to me, and nothing was really working." Initially she figured she didn't know enough, so she began to try what other salespeople in her company were doing at the time. But after several months of serious effort, she said, "I tried a bit of everything, and nothing seemed to work."

An Example of One of Julie's Early Ineffective Emails

(for confidentiality, we have changed some of the identifying details)

Hi Eric,

I manage the global relationship between Tech Systems and FranklinCovey. We've been doing leadership development work with other organizations structured like Tech Systems—organizations that have many operating companies underneath them—and I wanted to make you aware of a program that we created for organizations like Tech Systems. FranklinCovey has been offering all of our content to subsidiaries to access at a significantly reduced price per person. We call it All Access Pass. You may be familiar with some of our leadership offerings. Are you available to connect briefly on this? I can give you more information on the offering and share how we're working with other companies like Tech Systems.

I know each Tech Systems company operates independently so this may not be of interest to you. However, if you're looking for new and creative ways to offer world-class leadership development to Tech Systems employees, then I'd be happy to explore this with you and your team. If you would like to connect, then please let me know a good time.

Regards,
Julie Schmidt
Managing Director, Global Accounts

Frustrated but determined, she decided to start fresh and draw upon principles she knew worked. She asked herself, *How can I capture the attention of my client base and get them excited about new possibilities? What do they really need to know and experience? And how can I create enough interest to generate the right conversations, with the right people, which eventually will lead to success?* Her questions led her to use a framework we call a sales movie trailer.

MOVIE TRAILERS: TAKING A CUE FROM THE FILM INDUSTRY

As with billboards and the advertising industry, we were inspired to turn to the film industry to help salespeople become Strikingly Different in creating interest among their "audiences."

Through the medium of movie trailers, the film industry excels at capturing attention, creating interest, and motivating someone to act. What we've always appreciated about movie trailers is that studios invest staggering amounts of money in creating a film, employing hundreds of people as screenwriters, producers, cinematographers, costumers, grips, hair and makeup artists, choreographers, and many more. But the success of that movie—and the product of those people's years of work—is largely dependent on a two-minute movie trailer. With so much on the line, those two minutes are highly leveraged and carefully crafted frame by frame. Likewise, your organization invests heavily in marketing, research and development, talent development, product testing...yet your organization's success in the marketplace depends largely on the first few minutes you interact with clients. Folksy, cliché, or verbose approaches won't cut it. Like Julie, if you want to help decisive action take place, you could learn something from the movie industry.

CREATING SALES MOVIE TRAILERS

MOVIE TRAILERS ARE DESIGNED TO DO THREE THINGS REALLY WELL.

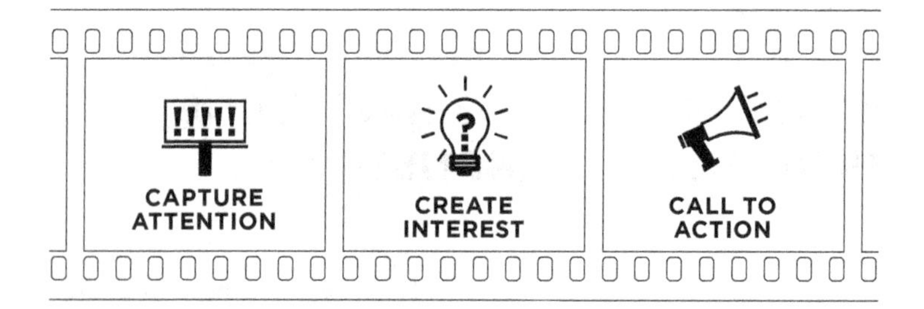

For sales purposes, we define a **movie trailer** as a brief verbal or written communication that excites the client or prospect to want to meet with you or intrigues the client at the start of a meeting or proposal so they actively engage in a peer-to-peer dialogue with you. To create a movie trailer, you'll take the main headline and three sub headlines of the billboard and develop them one step further.

Using a movie trailer to create interest contrasts with the Surprisingly Average approach of relying on jargon-heavy scripts, which quickly lose the client's interest and trigger resistance to your message.

With millions of dollars on the line, movie studios enlist neuroscientists to precisely measure which movie-trailer formulas are most predictive of box office sales, keeping their findings closely guarded secrets. Luckily, we don't have to be so secretive. Through our simulations and experience coaching thousands of salespeople, we've developed a straightforward and easily replicable framework for your movie trailers:

- **Capture attention** so your client or potential customer stops and listens. Your billboard main headline is a key part of capturing attention.

- **Create interest** in outcomes that would be beneficial or important to them and their company. Start with the sub headlines from your billboard and add just a couple of sentences for color and context to bring the movie trailer to life.
- Get their thoughts and then invite them to **take action**, either to meet with you (virtually or in person) or to engage fully in the meeting.

Contrast Julie's ineffective email earlier in the chapter with her successful email below that follows the "movie trailer" format. She chose to send emails that invited executives to attend exclusive live events, which later became live-online events. These events created an environment where executives could hear from global thought leaders on important topics related to current market challenges and learn more about her company's approach and potential solutions.

We understand you are likely in a different industry with a different message, so just pay attention to the principles she follows that you can use in your situation. Specifically, notice how she captures attention with a main headline, creates interest with From–To sub headlines and statements focused on the client's most important goals and issues, and calls the executives to action.

An Example of One of Julie's Early Effective Emails

(for confidentiality, we have changed some of the identifying details)

Subject: PLEASE RSVP: FranklinCovey Executive Event on February 6

Hi Stacey,

FranklinCovey is hosting an invitation-only executive event on February 6 from 8:30 a.m. - 11:30 a.m. at the HMS Conference Center in Anytown, USA. This complimentary session will feature internationally recognized thought leader and author Kory Kogon and will focus on **what sets leaders apart** at all levels of an organization.

Here is what we know: Your first-level leaders must transition **from "doing it themselves" to achieving results through others.** An unprecedented digitization of information and compression of management layers has made your **mid-to-senior-level leaders indispensable** and executive-level leaders must effectively set vision, execute strategy, and demonstrate personal trustworthiness to **create winning cultures.** Are all of your leaders ready?

What we will cover:

- FranklinCovey's Leadership Point of View: The Four Key Differentiators
- First-Level Leaders: The 6 Critical Practices for Leading a Team™
- Mid-to-Senior-Level Leaders: The 4 Essential Roles of Leadership®
- Executive-Level Leaders: Coaching and Feedback—The Lifeblood of the C-Suite

This event is limited to 100 invited business leaders and is already close to going on a wait list, so I am holding two seats for you. **Can you please let me know either way if you can attend and if there is anyone else you would like to bring?** My Inside Business Partner, Andrea, will get you registered if you can attend.

You can also view more information on the event here: www.franklincovey.com. Thank you and please let me know if you can attend!

Kind regards,

Julie Schmidt
Managing Director, Global Accounts

Julie found several points helpful in her experience. The people/lists she was sending to were *very* targeted—senior-level people who were decision makers and had titles that would care about and be interested in buying what she was selling (relevance). The email above was sent to an executive at a major products company. The client responded within a few hours and said she'd like to bring the head of another global department with her. This has become very typical for Julie.

Her subject (MAIN HEADLINE) of **PLEASE RSVP: FranklinCovey Executive Event on February 6** is intentional. The PLEASE RSVP in all caps captures the executive's attention so they will take the time to read the rest of the email. Julie has had CEOs and presidents respond to her emails...from their mobile devices.

The body of her message creates interest with From–To sub headlines and value statements focused on what likely matters most to the client executives. "Here is what we know: Your first-level leaders must transition FROM **'doing it themselves'** TO **'achieving results through others.'** An unprecedented digitization of information and compression of management layers has made your **mid-to-senior-level leaders indispensable** and executive-level leaders must effectively set vision, execute strategy, and demonstrate personal trustworthiness to **'create winning cultures.'** " Then she poses a thought-provoking question: Are all of your leaders ready?

She concluded the email with a call to action. Many executives responded by asking if they could reserve one or two more executive seats for their company. Other executives said, "I can't attend, but can I please send my colleague who is also a leader in our company?" And others said, "I can't attend but I am interested in attending at a different time."

Julie's emails created great interest and had such a high return of acceptance, she set up short pre-event meetings to gather information and prepare the executive to get the most out of the event. Following the event, she followed up with a pre-agreed upon meeting with each executive to discuss the topic further and find out where she and her company might be of help.

Julie found unique ways to capture the attention of her potential clients and create enough interest that they decided to act. Her approach became so successful, it is now used by numerous other salespeople across our organization.

Let's look at another successful movie trailer, this one taking place during a live phone call. The scenario: Jacob, a sales professional with National Printers, is calling Daniel, the COO of a manufacturing company. You'll notice this conversation is somewhat idealized to demonstrate the movie trailer framework; we've included tips on how to manage client resistance and obstacles in the section that follows.

Movie Trailer Example One

Scenario: Jacob, a sales professional with National Printers, is calling Daniel, the COO of a manufacturing company.

Jacob has done some research and learned that Daniel's company is a pioneer in developing and manufacturing robotic arms for the medical and aerospace industries. Jacob believes his company's 3D printing capabilities could really help Daniel's company achieve breakthrough results.

Jacob wants to talk with Daniel and get him interested in setting up a virtual demonstration of National Printers' 3D printing capabilities.

A movie trailer might go something like this:

Strikingly Different
MOVIE TRAILER ONE

CAPTURE ATTENTION

SALESPERSON: JACOB

WHY STRIKINGLY DIFFERENT?

CLIENT: DANIEL

Salesperson: Jacob	Why Strikingly Different?	Client: Daniel
Hello, Daniel, this is Jacob, from National Printers. Thanks for taking my call. ***I'll be brief. I lead our 3D printing business in this part of the country.***	**Jacob introduces himself with a client-facing title and lets the client know he will be brief.**	Hi, Jacob.
I've been following your company and am intrigued with your pioneering work developing robotic arms. ***You should be proud, especially with your latest innovation*** of embedding a supercomputer control system inside the robots.	**Jacob connects quickly and shows interest in the client's important work. He also demonstrates he has done research on the company and knows what he is talking about.**	Yes, we are really proud of what we've achieved to date. That was a huge breakthrough for us. I'm impressed you know that.
It was big news! I'm calling to see if you would be interested in some ideas we have to help you ***produce a custom robotic arm in just one day instead of a week.*** Could I take three minutes to share a little more information so you can decide whether it makes sense to set up another time to talk further?	**Jacob shares a compelling From–To HEADLINE focused on something that is relevant to the client. He then asks permission to keep talking and lets Daniel know the decision to be made after he has shared some more information.**	That's intriguing. Yes, please go ahead and tell me more.

Strikingly Different
MOVIE TRAILER ONE

SALESPERSON: JACOB

WHY **STRIKINGLY DIFFERENT?**

CLIENT: DANIEL

I read your latest press release, and ***it sounds like you are starting to explore new technologies*** to help you increase precision and shorten production time. Based on 3D printing work we've done with other advanced robotics companies, ***you can likely cut your production time from 7 days to 1 day, lower your costs, and increase quality with a different process. Would it be helpful to give you one cut deeper on how you could do that?***

Jacob shares a little more information, does a subtle call-out to work done with other companies, and then connects back to the main From-To HEADLINE he used to capture Daniel's attention along with two additional ideas.

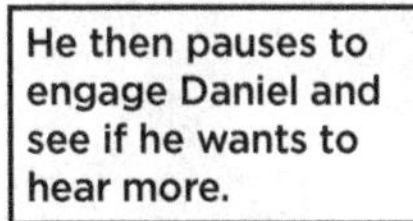

He then pauses to engage Daniel and see if he wants to hear more.

Yes, we are looking for ways to cut production time and lower costs.

The big ideas are *first,* you can use a new carbon fiber material that is stronger and more precise, allowing you to ***go from 700+ parts to less than 100 for each arm. Second,*** the fewer, higher quality parts will ***drive dramatic reductions in your material and labor costs with low defect rates and less rework.*** And *third,* your ***ROI on the new technology is typically recovered in a single output.***

Jacob introduces three compelling SUB HEADLINES. In this instance, Jacob decides to share a bit of the "how" along with the resulting outcomes. For a COO, this would be highly relevant.

Jacob creates clear contrast between Daniel's current situation and a compelling future state achieved by working together.

Yes, please go on.

Strikingly Different
MOVIE TRAILER ONE

CALL TO ACTION

SALESPERSON: JACOB

WHY STRIKINGLY DIFFERENT?

CLIENT: DANIEL

Jacob: Daniel, what are your thoughts?

← **Jacob confirms Daniel's interest.**

Daniel: Well, it sounds fantastic, and almost too good to be true. I want to talk further.

Jacob transfers motivation to the client.

Jacob: Great! Let's compare calendars and set up 60 minutes soon to dive into the details. Would it be helpful to give you a demo of the 3D printing technology as part of our conversation?

← **Jacob sets up a second meeting.**

Daniel: Yes, I would really like to see the technology and then discuss specifically how we can apply it to our manufacturing process to achieve the outcomes you mentioned.

I'm really looking forward to talking with you again next week.

The client is leaning in and wants to see the demo. →

Jacob: I'm excited to show you the technology and brainstorm the best ways to use it in your environment.

Have a great day.

Daniel: Goodbye.
[End of call]

Remember to think and speak in headlines, but when it comes to a movie trailer, your goal is different: It's not just to capture attention, it's to *create interest*. So, build out your sub headlines or From–To statements. Add nuance to show that you understand their goals, where their trouble is, and how you can help. Bring in emotion around the challenges you know are going on in the organization. In this example, we've expanded the From–To statements from the billboard. There's more to them now, and that's intentional—they need to be substantial and intriguing enough to *elicit a reaction.* A few tips for delivering your movie trailer:

- Deliver the movie trailer early because you want the client to know what you're going to be talking about.
- Expand the billboard to make it even more relevant, distinct, and memorable, but limit yourself to no more than two or three key ideas. Any more is too much for a single interaction.
- If you're speaking live, obtain permission to take a short time to connect. Most of us hate to do this because we think we're going to be stopped. But it rarely happens if you have a decent headline and well-crafted introduction. There will be resistance and a bit of tension—that's the protective filter in their brains that is working hard to keep them safe. But by saying, "Can I take ninety seconds to share what we talked about/to get your reaction/to decide whether or not you think we should meet?" and honoring that commitment, the client is more likely to lower their resistance and actually listen—at least for the next ninety seconds.
- When you deliver the full movie trailer, slow down slightly. Not rushing communicates that you're engaging peer to peer. Frantically cramming in your ideas as the seconds tick by can make you seem "less than" the client.

CUSTOMIZE AND EVOLVE YOUR MOVIE TRAILER

Just as movie studios create dozens of versions of movie trailers for various audiences and countries, you'll develop several movie trailers as you meet with different people throughout a client organization. What an IT director finds relevant, distinctive, or interesting likely differs from what a chief human resource officer thinks, so you'll need to adjust your movie trailer accordingly. Movie trailers should also evolve as we move through the sales cycle, understand more about the client's situation, and gain real data points from them.

Sound complicated? Remember that the framework of the movie trailer is to capture attention, create and increase interest, then deliver a call to action. If those three simple elements stay in your mind, you can flexibly add, delete, and modify statements to make it more relevant, distinct, and memorable.

Aim for Action

A movie trailer isn't worth much unless it can incite action. We can't promise that every time you use a movie trailer, you're going to get a positive reaction any more than with actual movie trailers. But the most important part is don't sell them—ask. Don't push—start a dialogue. How do we do that? Remember that we've asked the client if we could take ninety seconds to see whether or not they think you should meet or whether this has created enough interest. So after we share our movie trailer, ask that very question: "I'm curious if any part of what I shared makes sense to you." Use an open-ended question, *not* a yes or a no—we want dialogue. Then, "It sounds like maybe we should meet" or "It sounds like we're on target for this meeting" or "Would it make sense for us to get another meeting here with the CTO?"

Gathering Information to Create a Movie Trailer

When you're addressing new customers, you may not know what the problem statements are or what will resonate with them. So how do you create an initial opener?

If you have colleagues who may know that particular organization, team, or line of business, or who work in other areas of that same organization, you can bounce ideas off them and have them coach you. But if you don't know anyone, you can still create a movie trailer. No matter who you're talking to, one of the most common things clients are going to ask is "Can you tell me about your experience? Where have you done things like this in the past, or what have you noticed with other insurers/healthcare organizations/etc.?" You can do research to get close, but the best source of information is your past experience with other clients. Using your past experience and talking with colleagues or people within that organization are safe bets, because no one is expecting you to know more, given the fact that you're outside the organization. Those are not only practical places to play, but you can generally take those to the bank with most executives.

You can't be certain that every detail in your movie trailer will match their situation, *and that's OK.* As long as you're directionally correct on the topic, application, business metrics, timing, etc., the client usually will have enough to react to. Remember, the whole key here is to create dialogue. The reason you're doing some of these things isn't because you want to demonstrate that you know everything. It's to put ideas forward to say, "Let's get into this."

HOW TO USE MOVIE TRAILERS

In the previous sections, we've shown how you can use movie trailers to get a meeting, but they can be effective throughout the sales cycle. In fact, the movie trailer doesn't have to be used in a conversation at all. We can use the movie trailer in the form of an email, a written document, or a short text. We've even used this through LinkedIn as an inbox message. To be clear, the term "movie trailer" isn't one you would use with a client. The subject of your email shouldn't be: *Here's My Movie Trailer!* Your subject line should be the main headline from your billboard: in the case of earlier examples, "Cut the time to make resource decisions from > four weeks to < two hours" or "Deploy new infrastructure in hours/days, not weeks/months."

Let's look at three situations throughout the sales cycle where you could use a movie trailer.

Connect With a New Contact or Pass Through a Gatekeeper

When you don't know the person you want to meet with, use this pattern:

- Provide your name.
- Give your title using client-focused, not internal, phrasing.
- Acknowledge your connection, if any.
- Ask for permission (enable the "no").

It might sound something like this: "This is Kathy Williams from Assure; I lead our business transformation practice here in Illinois. I was speaking with Anthony Walker the other day about [this is where we would insert our main headline], and he thought we might want to talk. Do you have a couple minutes for me to share what Anthony and I discussed, so you can determine whether we should meet?"

Particularly with new clients, we've found we can't often access an executive without working through the administrative or executive assistant. Movie trailers work well in this situation: "My name is Leela Young from Ascend, and I lead our financial services practice in EMEA. I've been wanting to have a quick online meeting with Cameron, and I know you work directly with her. Could I take ninety seconds and share what I think would be of value to her and get your reaction?" Then let them weigh in on the movie trailer. Work with assistants as partners.

Gain Buy-In on a Meeting Agenda

Have you ever been in an online meeting in which you're expecting two people from the client to be there, and all of a sudden, a third shows up, someone you've never met before? In the "old" days, someone dropping in on a conference room meeting would happen only occasionally, but we're finding that we encounter unexpected attendees more frequently online. So, could a movie trailer be helpful in this now-common situation? Absolutely. It could be as simple as, "Priya, it's nice to meet you. As we're talking through this, our end in mind today is to review some of our experience and solutions, so that by the end of the time together, you can decide whether or not we should invest more time in a solution. So Priya, could I give you a short recap of what the main themes are and where we're at, just to make sure that we're headed in the right direction for you?" Then deliver your movie trailer to bring uniformity to what you're trying to do in the meeting and get people heading in the same direction.

Conclude a Meeting With a Punch to Earn the Next Meeting

Besides kicking off meetings, movie trailers can be used to pull everything together at the end of a meeting. Particularly in an early stage of the sales cycle, you've often been exploring divergent thinking and have a lot of "stuff on the table," some of which has worked and some that hasn't. Conclude the meeting with the bare bones version of a movie trailer (i.e., just the relevant From–To sub headlines) by saying something like, "Why don't I take a crack at summing up what we've talked about over the last forty-five minutes? I think what we're saying is..." Deliver your movie trailer (sharing just the relevant From–To sub headlines that resonated with the client), then ask for decisive action: "Should we sponsor a meeting with the CMO? Should we do a business case together? Do you see enough differentiation here that you'd be willing to downselect us?"

MORE MOVIE TRAILER EXAMPLES

Let's walk through an example of how to use a movie trailer format to interest a client. This example contrasts a Surprisingly Average movie trailer (i.e., ineffective) with a Strikingly Different movie trailer (i.e., relevant, distinct, and memorable). As you read this, think of how you might craft a movie trailer for your clients, using your own style, and in your own way. For simplicity, the salesperson in this example is making a phone call to the prospect, but this framework can be adapted to any medium, including emails, social media, texts, etc.

Movie Trailer Example Two

1

CAPTURE ATTENTION

2

CREATE INTEREST

3

CALL TO ACTION

SALESPERSON:
CHANTE

CLIENT:
MICHELLE

Scenario: Chante, a sales professional with a consulting firm, is about to get on a brief introductory call with Michelle, the CIO of a digital services company.

Chante has talked with a couple of employees that work for Michelle, including Jon Golden, over the past two weeks. Jon explained the following:

- The organization has been inundated with back-office maintenance requests for a long time.
- The top performers in Information Technology (IT) want to play a more strategic role in the growth of the company, but they are overwhelmed with just keeping up.
- The CIO wants to change that and elevate IT's role by 1) making IT more relevant to the business, 2) outsourcing application maintenance and development, and 3) cutting costs.

Chante wants to get a more in-depth meeting with the CIO to share insights and see if it makes sense to talk further.

Remember, the first dialogue below is a Surprisingly Average example.

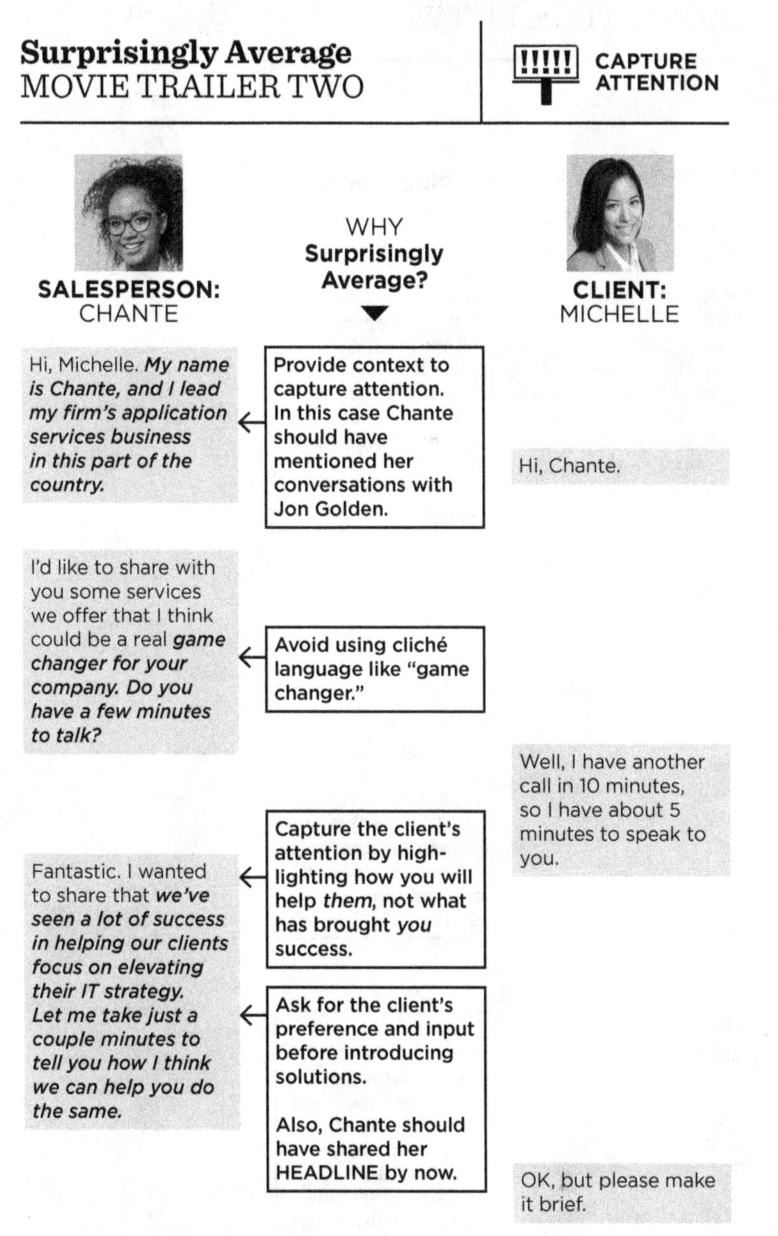

Surprisingly Average
MOVIE TRAILER TWO

CREATE INTEREST

SALESPERSON: CHANTE

WHY **Surprisingly Average?**

CLIENT: MICHELLE

Chante: I spoke to Jon Golden from your organization, and he let me know that you're trying to manage a huge number of system maintenance requests. We've helped many other companies with this issue. And I'm sure we can help you too.

Why: This conversation is really lagging without a HEADLINE. Michelle still isn't sure how Chante can help. And mentioning Jon Golden this far into the conversation feels awkward.

Michelle: It's nice to know you're familiar with one of our challenges. But what IT services do you offer?

Chante: I am confident we can help you drive business growth, implement outsourcing to deploy applications more quickly, and reduce your costs.

Why: This list of services is vague and will not create interest. Chante should present From–To SUB HEADLINES that include symptoms, outcomes, emotions, or a combination of all three.

Michelle: I have to admit, that all sounds great. But it seems like a huge commitment. How will you do it? I've trusted other service providers in the past, and I ended up disappointed.

Chante: I'm really excited about the possibilities for your company because I've seen great results with several other clients we've worked with recently. I'll send you a copy of those numbers so you can see what we did.

Why: This response tells Michelle that Chante is not listening and is not really concerned about her organization's challenges. Chante is still focused on herself and her solution, not on what Michelle and her organization need.

Surprisingly Average MOVIE TRAILER TWO

CALL TO ACTION

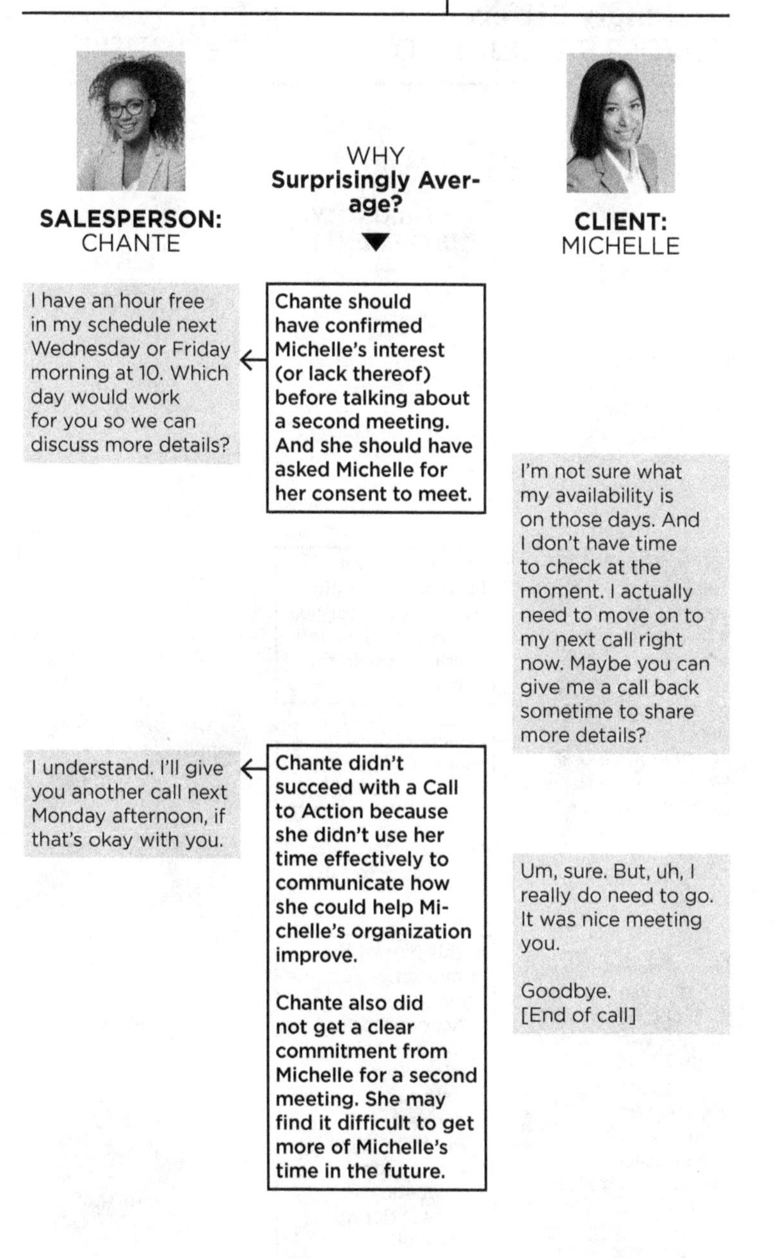

SALESPERSON: CHANTE

WHY **Surprisingly Average?**

CLIENT: MICHELLE

Chante: I have an hour free in my schedule next Wednesday or Friday morning at 10. Which day would work for you so we can discuss more details?

Chante should have confirmed Michelle's interest (or lack thereof) before talking about a second meeting. And she should have asked Michelle for her consent to meet.

Michelle: I'm not sure what my availability is on those days. And I don't have time to check at the moment. I actually need to move on to my next call right now. Maybe you can give me a call back sometime to share more details?

Chante: I understand. I'll give you another call next Monday afternoon, if that's okay with you.

Chante didn't succeed with a Call to Action because she didn't use her time effectively to communicate how she could help Michelle's organization improve.

Chante also did not get a clear commitment from Michelle for a second meeting. She may find it difficult to get more of Michelle's time in the future.

Michelle: Um, sure. But, uh, I really do need to go. It was nice meeting you.

Goodbye.
[End of call]

The next dialogue is a *good* example. It is Strikingly Different. Notice the contrast between the previous dialogue and this one.

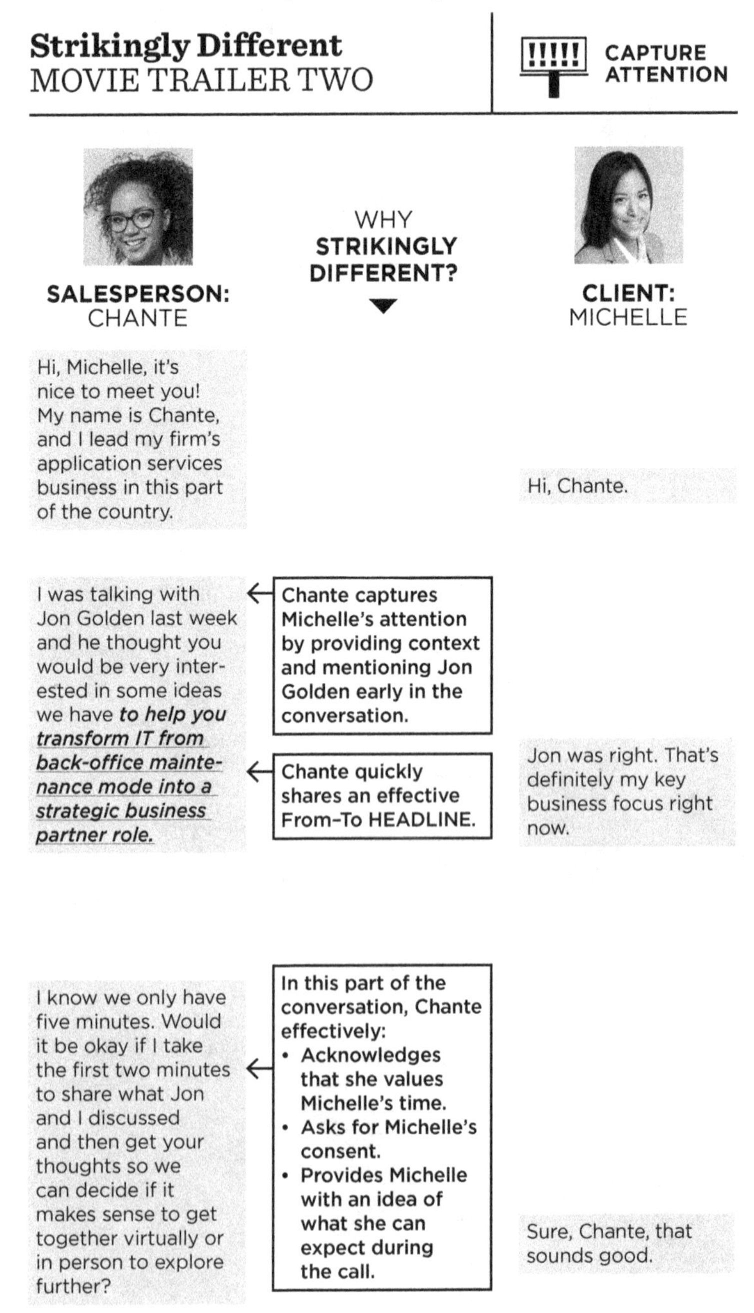

Strikingly Different
MOVIE TRAILER TWO

!!!!! **CAPTURE ATTENTION**

SALESPERSON: CHANTE	WHY **STRIKINGLY DIFFERENT?**	**CLIENT:** MICHELLE
Hi, Michelle, it's nice to meet you! My name is Chante, and I lead my firm's application services business in this part of the country.		Hi, Chante.
I was talking with Jon Golden last week and he thought you would be very interested in some ideas we have ***to help you transform IT from back-office maintenance mode into a strategic business partner role.***	**Chante captures Michelle's attention by providing context and mentioning Jon Golden early in the conversation.** **Chante quickly shares an effective From-To HEADLINE.**	Jon was right. That's definitely my key business focus right now.
I know we only have five minutes. Would it be okay if I take the first two minutes to share what Jon and I discussed and then get your thoughts so we can decide if it makes sense to get together virtually or in person to explore further?	**In this part of the conversation, Chante effectively:** • **Acknowledges that she values Michelle's time.** • **Asks for Michelle's consent.** • **Provides Michelle with an idea of what she can expect during the call.**	Sure, Chante, that sounds good.

Strikingly Different
MOVIE TRAILER TWO

SALESPERSON: CHANTE

WHY **STRIKINGLY DIFFERENT?**

CLIENT: MICHELLE

Chante: Jon mentioned the IT organization is working furiously right now to keep up with a never-ending stream of system maintenance requests. And that work burden is keeping you from achieving your vision of elevating IT and being a lot more strategic for the business. We've seen that same scenario in many other organizations, and I imagine it is very frustrating.

Why strikingly different? Chante shares what she already knows about the organization and builds client trust.

Chante also gives Michelle a chance to confirm that what she is sharing about her organizational goals is correct.

Michelle: You have no idea. I'm at my wits end. Please go on.

Chante: Well, we've been analyzing your situation and believe it is possible for you to achieve your strategic vision and do three things you're not able to do today within the next 12 months: ***First,* redeploy your top IT talent from maintenance problem solvers to business growth drivers; *second,* test and deploy your applications in hours/days not weeks/months** with an innovative outsourcing model; and ***third,* cut IT costs by 35% and reinvest the difference** into targeted opportunities to grow the business.

Why strikingly different? Chante introduces three From-To SUBHEADLINES. She creates clear contrast between Michelle's current situation and a future state achieved by working with Chante.

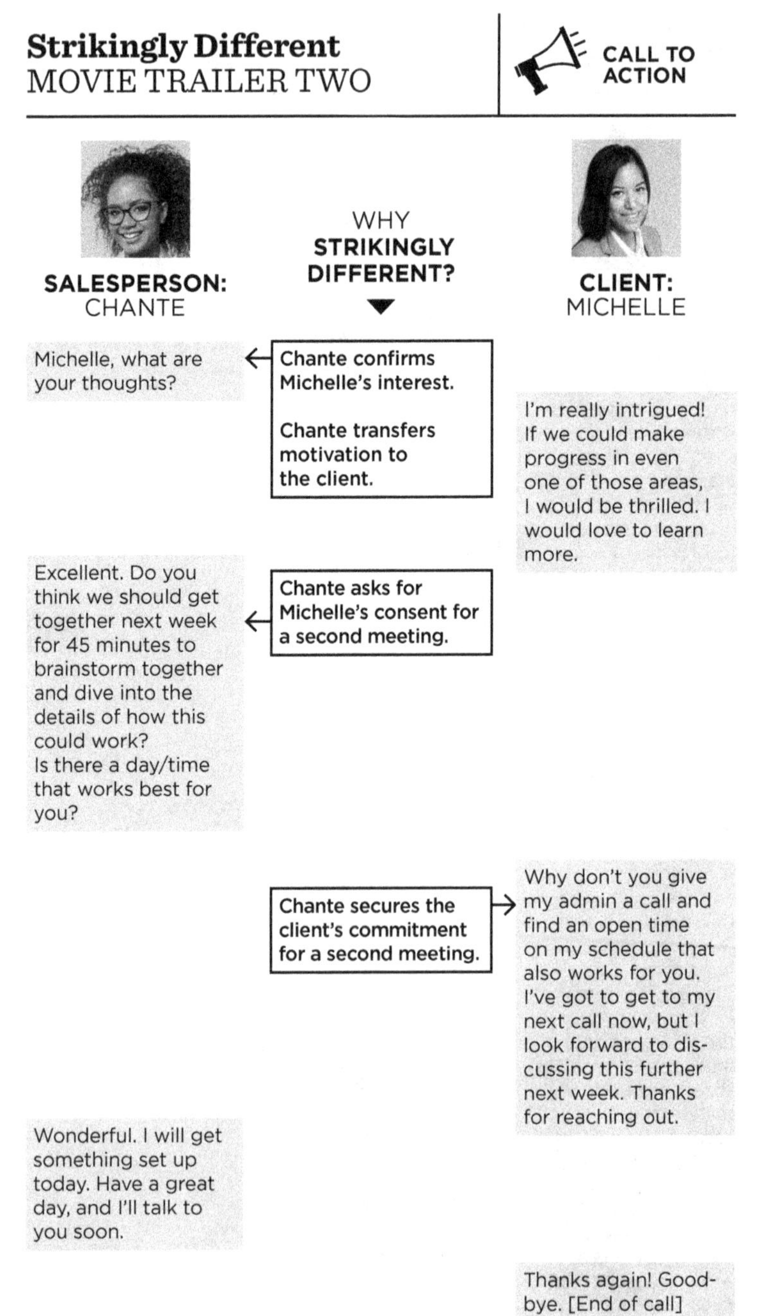
Strikingly Different
MOVIE TRAILER TWO
CALL TO ACTION
SALESPERSON: CHANTE
WHY STRIKINGLY DIFFERENT?
CLIENT: MICHELLE
Michelle, what are your thoughts?
Chante confirms Michelle's interest.
Chante transfers motivation to the client.
I'm really intrigued! If we could make progress in even one of those areas, I would be thrilled. I would love to learn more.
Excellent. Do you think we should get together next week for 45 minutes to brainstorm together and dive into the details of how this could work? Is there a day/time that works best for you?
Chante asks for Michelle's consent for a second meeting.
Chante secures the client's commitment for a second meeting.
Why don't you give my admin a call and find an open time on my schedule that also works for you. I've got to get to my next call now, but I look forward to discussing this further next week. Thanks for reaching out.
Wonderful. I will get something set up today. Have a great day, and I'll talk to you soon.
Thanks again! Goodbye. [End of call]

Create a movie trailer for an upcoming meeting, and share it with a colleague, then ask for feedback. Did the movie trailer capture attention? Did it create interest? Did you make an effective call to action?

Once you've raised the clients' level of excitement through movie trailers, you need to assure them that you have the experience and ability to help them achieve those results. In the next chapter, we'll show you how to build that confidence and trust.

KEY INSIGHTS FOR SKILL 2

- Understand the definition and purpose of a Sales Movie Trailer: a brief verbal or written communication that excites the client or prospect to want to meet with you, intrigues the client at the start of a meeting or proposal so they actively engage in a peer-to-peer dialogue with you, or earns you an invitation for another meeting.
    - You capture attention by using the main headline from your billboard, along with brief contextual information.
    - You create interest by highlighting something beneficial or important to the client and their organization.
    - You extend a call to action by first listening and understanding the client's needs and then extending an invitation (such as meeting with you virtually or engaging actively in a face-to-face meeting).

Skill 3:
BUILD CONFIDENCE WITH FLASHBACKS AND FLASHFORWARDS

Strikingly Different Message House

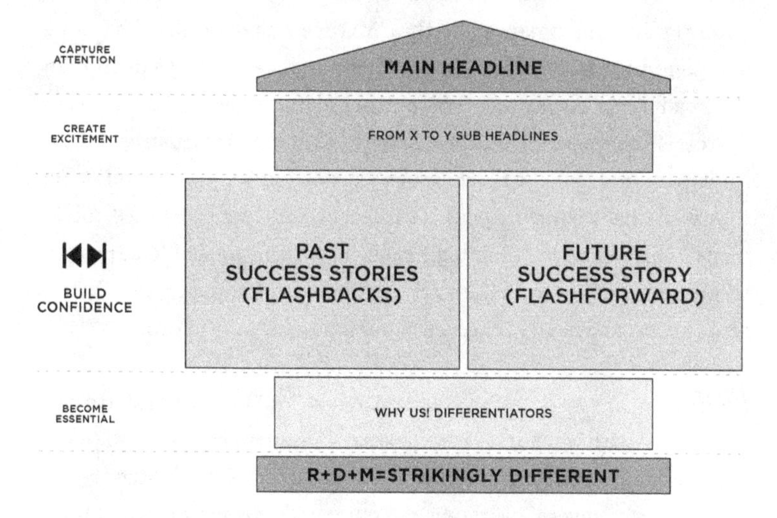

One of the most common questions clients ask is "So where have you done this before?" To have confidence in your insights and solutions, your clients need to know you have credible prior experience. The challenge is how do you bring your past experience forward and make it relevant and meaningful without yakking on too long?

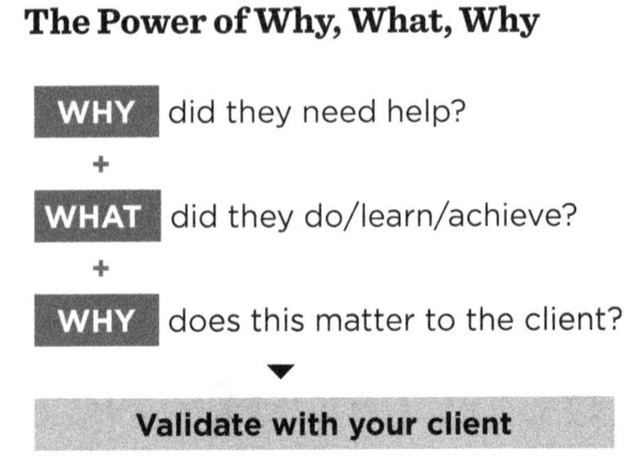

Here is a brief story that is a composite of our clients' experience in Europe. Dominique, a sales executive at a French company that specialized in optimizing retail operations, was meeting with a potential new customer, Adele, the CMO at a global retailer of clothing and general merchandise. Adele's company was seeing a decline in their same-store sales, and their online business was shrinking due to aggressive competition. Adele expressed a high level of frustration that their attempts to solve these issues weren't working fast enough. As they were discussing the possible release of an upcoming RFP, Adele mentioned that one of their biggest selection criteria would be proven retail experience. Adele then asked, "What is your experience in the retail space, and have you solved challenges like ours before?"

Dominique answered, "I'm glad you asked, and I'd love to share our experience with you. First, let me just say I'm sorry you are having such significant challenges right now. I've been working with other retail customers for several years, and the current environment is certainly challenging. Here's the good news: we have seen new opportunities for companies who take advantage of the changing trends and offer consumers what they're seeking. I think the best way to illustrate our experience is to tell you about a similar customer situation where we helped them **move from double-digit same-store sales declines to positive growth in twelve months**. I'll briefly share why they needed help, what we did and achieved, and why that could make a real difference for you. Then, we can talk more in depth about your situation and explore whether we can help you overcome your current challenges and achieve higher revenue.

"The customer was another major European retailer based in Paris whose situation was very similar to yours. They were experiencing same-store sales declines that were actually worse than you described. They were also struggling to get their online business to grow due to very stiff competition, so they needed results as fast as possible.

"That meant we had to move quickly. We applied a proprietary analytical approach that highlighted a significant opportunity to increase in-store and online sales by harnessing social media and mobile phone use. There were a lot of details, of course, but the short story is we implemented an end-to-end mobile solution for in-store, online, and mobile shopping in just twelve months. The client went on to see their in-store sales grow by nearly 3 percent and their online sales by more than 23 percent in twelve months. In addition, they now have the tools to stay current with trends and analyze buying behaviors. Given our experience, I believe it may be possible for you to realize similar results in turning around your in-store and online sales. Is that the type of experience you're looking for?"

Dominique's response to her client's question was brief and thoughtful (note how she showed empathy before sharing the flashback). It was more effective than listing the names of three companies she had done work with recently because it feels authentic and focused on what the customer is really asking, which is "Can you help us turn things around?"

So how do you answer that frequently asked question, "Where have you done this before?" Are you prepared with an example or two to share with potential clients when they ask that question? We're sure it's no surprise to you that to have confidence in your insights and solutions, your clients need to understand your prior experience. But what did surprise us was just how many salespeople are unprepared or don't share their experience in a way that clients find helpful. *What* you say, along with *how* you share your past experience, will make all the difference in whether or not you actually build that confidence and credibility.

What's surprising to most salespeople is that clients *don't want a lot of depth* in stories about our experience, at least at this point. They want the context, the results, and the relevance to their situation—then *they* want to respond. Clients are asking you to set the table, not give them the full buffet. Why? Because this is only the starting part of a larger discussion, and they, the executives, want to drive it. They don't want us driving it. And that's good news because if they're driving, they're engaged.

Based on this feedback, we created a very simple formula that has since been shown over and over again to be what clients want. It's a powerful way to share both past success stories and, using the same format, a future success story that involves the prospective client. We call these story forms "flashbacks" and "flashforwards."

SHARING FLASHBACKS WITH THE WHY, WHAT, WHY FRAMEWORK

In sales, a **flashback** is an account of a past achievement or performance of a person, organization, or solution. It provides proof of results and establishes that you're credible. To stay concise and relevant, these success stories are best portrayed using a Why, What, Why format.

Instead of droning on about how incredible you, your company, and your solutions are, tell a flashback success story from the perspective of a past client to illustrate how your differences helped them achieve success. Then relate those differences to the prospective client, sharing that it's the right story because you can directly relate that prior success to their needs and situation.

Let's take another example based on a flashback from a successful, real-life client interaction (again, to maintain confidentiality, we have changed some specifics). Imagine you're exploring whether to work with a global hospitality company with $10 billion in revenue, across fifteen resorts and 60,000 employees. They've been dealing with external pressure to improve performance and have ineffective analytics models and disconnected processes. The client asks, "Have you done anything like this before?"

Transition

SURPRISINGLY AVERAGE	STRIKINGLY DIFFERENT
Sure. We do a lot of work in the hospitality industry. In the past eighteen months, we successfully delivered projects with three of the largest hospitality players.	I'm glad you asked me that question. As we've been talking about your challenges, I couldn't help but think about another client in a similar situation who we recently helped achieve some pretty remarkable results. I'd like to briefly share why they needed help, what we did and achieved, and why I think that matters to you. Then we can explore the situation a bit more in depth wherever you would like, to see if it makes sense for us to keep talking.

While IQ is essential when sharing credible stories—rigor, critical thinking, creative thinking, the ability to adapt, and so forth—EQ or emotional quotient allows you to gracefully connect the flashback to the conversation and avoid a jarring non sequitur.

Transition statements are always important to build context, but they are absolutely essential when using an example from a different industry or vertical. Do not surprise clients by drawing from another industry without first giving them a heads-up. If you're talking to an insurance company and you share an example from retail, the client will be more focused on wondering why you're sharing a seemingly irrelevant example than listening to the actual story. But if you clarify the reason you're putting this on the table, you can keep the client's attention focused where you want it to be: "As we were walking through your scenario, I couldn't stop thinking about a client in a different area of financial services" or "It caught my attention that we've had some great experience in retail using similar technology to drive greater customer change. I recognize it's not your industry, but I think this could be very helpful for you for two reasons. One, we've done a ton of this work, so you get the expertise we have, and two, you would be breaking ground in your competitive environment. So can I walk you through that experience for a minute, even though it's a different industry, and then we can talk about where it would mesh?"

Using that transition, you have someone sitting up in their seat, leaning forward, and saying, "OK, I don't know if this is going to work, but lay it on me." That's far better than if you just subtly bounced it past them.

The First Why

SURPRISINGLY AVERAGE	STRIKINGLY DIFFERENT
We have twenty years of experience working with three of the top global hotel chains. We've had great success, and I'm sure we can help.	One of our clients was another large hospitality company. They too were under a lot of pressure to improve their operating performance and their analytic models. They needed to turn things around.

This section should also be relatively brief—quickly deliver context for why the previous client engaged your organization. Talk about the business issues and outcomes, not about technology or specific processes.

What

SURPRISINGLY AVERAGE	STRIKINGLY DIFFERENT
What we have found successful recently with several hotels is to standardize and automate their call center operations. This upgrading of their centers begins with a set of best practices brought by our global consulting team. We standardize all of the centers on a single platform utilizing our proven "connect technology." As a result, we can align all center operations under a centralized operating model, leading to exciting cost savings. Next using our patented digital automation program, we transition their manual booking procedures into a fast, secure, and error-free reservation system—resulting in increases in efficiency, productivity, and happier guests. Clients love our approach.	So we conducted a digital strategy assessment and developed a comprehensive roadmap to achieve their future state vision. Three aspects of the engagement strike me as being spot on with your situation. Number one, we set up an analytics center of excellence and found opportunities to reinvest in their data supply chain. The second thing was we created a digital solution for push-pull reporting from a common set of data and metrics, and finally we developed a data supply chain operating model to enhance quality, security, and access. They've achieved $20 million in annual savings, reduced management reports from an incredible 4,000 to just 60 unique reports, and identified another $315 million in profitable growth opportunities.

In this case, we said there were three aspects we wanted to discuss. Don't go much past three; it takes too long for the client to jump in. You can always add another element later when you're having your discussion, but in the flashback itself, pick the two or three that are the best fit for that client. Often, you'll have to change these depending on who you're talking to in the organization and what's going on for them.

Again, you're trying to set the table so that the client has ideas to respond to. Some of these talking points may not be as important as others for them, and you want to gauge which ones pique their interest.

Remember to use real numbers here, if at all possible: real percentages, real timelines. You can always be a little conservative if you need to be.

The Second Why

SURPRISINGLY AVERAGE	STRIKINGLY DIFFERENT
As you can see, we have great technology, a talented team of consultants, and proven processes, creating outstanding results.	As you might imagine, our client was thrilled with the results they achieved, and our deep experience and unique strategy made a difference in helping them get those results. Now, while we haven't analyzed your specific situation in great detail, I believe after just our short conversation that it's very likely you could realize similar positive results in [*notice we're inserting a headline here*] improving your operating performance, becoming more data-driven, and connecting your processes and your people.

Many salespeople take this last why for granted. It seems that they're hoping the clients make the connection on their own, but we really do need to spell out why this story relates to them. You might start with caveats depending on the stage of the sales cycle you're in. For early stage: "We haven't spent a lot of time together yet..." or if you're mid-stage, "Although I've had conversations with several people, this isn't in cement yet, but I feel like this may be heading in a good direction." If you're in the final stage, there are no caveats. You can be bold: "Given our experience here, we think they're directly related in these ways..."

In any case, while you're having these conversations, you want to ask that final question: "What are your thoughts?" or another open-ended question. Your goal isn't to wrap up the conversation in a nice little bow; it's to further the conversation.

BEST PRACTICES FOR USING THE WHY, WHAT, WHY FRAMEWORK

1. **Set the table for further discussion**. Keep your message initially tight, three to four minutes long. This will take practice and focus; it is very easy to talk on and on for ten-plus minutes and not realize it.
2. **Stay away from the how.** Don't unnecessarily expand the framework. Notice that the "how" is missing from this framework, and that's one hundred percent intentional. Very rarely are clients interested in details of another organization implementing your solutions—they might want those details eventually, but not at this point.
3. **Don't skip the final why.** One of the fatal flaws when salespeople share a case or their own experience is that this last why is typically missing. Most of us just make the assumption, *Oh, they'll get the point.* But we found after watching thousands of these interactions that clients *don't* make the connection, or at least they don't make the connection the way you wanted them to.
4. **Pass the mic to the client.** Most sellers tend to go on too long, and we're not kidding—we mean two to three times past the point when clients are sending nonverbals for them to stop talking. The client is communicating, "I got it. Hey, we're good, we're good." But we're like, "Wait, there's more!" If we're working with a team, this problem is even worse because after we've done our piece, our colleagues want to jump in and do theirs. And the client is saying, "Hey folks, you hit the mark. Stop selling, stop pushing. I'm there." We often think credibility comes from a lengthy story that goes into great depth, and that's just not true. It comes from dialogue *with* the client.
5. **Validate to begin the true conversation.** The last piece is to validate with your client so you can really begin the discussion. Learn what made sense to them, what didn't, what worked, and what didn't work. Remember: the client's reaction is the main reason for this discussion.

Let's give this simple yet powerful framework a try. Create a flashback for an upcoming meeting, and practice it with a colleague, then ask for feedback. Did it take less than three to four minutes to share? Did you end by soliciting a response from your colleague? Was it relevant, distinct, and memorable?

SHARING FLASHFORWARDS WITH THE WHY, WHAT, WHY FRAMEWORK

A **flashforward** is a story of a possible future for the prospective client, focusing on different and better outcomes and results.

Flashbacks and flashforwards are two different sides of the same coin. With flashbacks, you're looking back to where you've helped other clients in similar situations achieve remarkable results. And when you flip the coin, you're looking into the future, with a flashforward on how this particular client can achieve those results and what the journey may look like for them.

FLASHBACK	FLASHFORWARD
• A record of past achievements or performance of a person, organization, or solution. • Answers the question "Where have you done this before?" • Provides proof of results. • Establishes that YOU are credible.	• A story for the future. • An exciting vision of what the client can do and achieve with you. • Focuses on how THEY will get the different/better outcomes and results. • Connects the WHY with the WHAT and the HOW.

For flashforwards, we use the same pattern of Why, What, Why, just applied differently.

Why, What, Why

FLASHBACK	FLASHFORWARD
WHY did they need to change?	WHY do you need to change?
WHAT did they do/learn/achieve?	WHAT is the journey?
WHY does this story matter?	WHY do this?

Let's see a flashforward in action, used by a customer relationship management platform company in a live-online meeting during the COVID-19 pandemic.

Here's the context: You're talking with a prospect from a large federal agency with multiple regional offices. The agency has been dealing with pressure to open their offices. You shared some insights that really connected with the prospect. You can tell the energy in the meeting is high, and the prospect is leaning into the conversation. Toward the end of the conversation, the prospect asks, "Can you give me a big-picture view of how you might approach this with us?"

You would begin with a transition statement to set up your Why, What, Why, saying something like this:

Transition

SURPRISINGLY AVERAGE	STRIKINGLY DIFFERENT
Sure, here are a few thoughts.	I'd be happy to. Let me summarize what the journey would look like at a high level, and why this approach would provide you with better outcomes now and prepare you for the future more effectively than other alternatives you may be considering. If that resonates, then we can talk about what makes sense to do next.

First Why

SURPRISINGLY AVERAGE	STRIKINGLY DIFFERENT
[Surprisingly Average sellers often skip the first why and tend to jump right into the "what" with solutions, sequencing, and timing.]	Opening your offices too soon or haphazardly could introduce a lot of risk to your employees, your constituents, and your organization's ability to operate effectively. The care you take in opening can build confidence and affect the judgments people make about your leadership. A misstep can wipe it away in an instant, so the stakes are high.

What

SURPRISINGLY AVERAGE	STRIKINGLY DIFFERENT
We would come in and run an app to figure out how ready your employees are for the change. We would then train them and update your emergency response management approach. The project would probably take six months to complete, depending on how much of the work your staff can do.	Based on our discussion and experience with other agencies, we would like to help you identify a process now so you can establish parameters for opening offices safely and also start identifying regions that meet those parameters. From our experience, this will probably be a three-phase project and will likely take around six months to complete, depending on how much your staff can help. The phase work includes an app to assess employee and workplace readiness, reskilling employees as necessary, and establishing an up-to-date emergency response management approach to lower future risk to achieving a successful mission.

Second Why

SURPRISINGLY AVERAGE	STRIKINGLY DIFFERENT
We've had really good success doing these types of projects with other agencies. It will make a big difference for you.	The outcomes you can expect are worth the journey. You should see a reduction of employee absenteeism from 17 percent to as low as 8 percent, nearly doubling your agency's efficiency. And, instead of your employees wondering if they are at risk of becoming ill, they'll be able to focus on their work. Let me pause and get your reaction to what I've shared.

At this point, you pause and find out what the client is thinking. Did that story resonate? What do they think about the potential to get the outcomes you mentioned?

In this example, you could use specific efficiency percentages because you experienced similar outcomes when working with other agencies in the past year. And given a similar profile, the prospective client could likely be in that range, as well. Just be conservative; make sure the numbers are credible.

The flashforward is about getting the client excited about the journey and the destination, and it allows you to pretest key elements of the solution. A flashforward could come up as early as the first meeting for a simple pursuit or might not come up until later in a more complicated sale.

Regardless of the stage you're in, as soon as the client shows sufficient interest, the flashforward *changes* from a high-level story to an iterative process where you and the client work together to co-create a solution that exactly meets their needs. This typically involves several meetings, design workshops, demos, and other efforts that will ultimately lead to a compelling, customized final proposal. (We'll discuss co-creating in more detail in Part 2.)

When a flashforward comes up, you have a chance to take what you've learned from the client in your conversation and help them become excited about their own journey—what it looks like, why they need to go on it, and what will happen as a result.

We often flash back so we can flash forward. By sharing past outcomes, we build the client's confidence that we can replicate a similar approach and success for them, even when they may have different goals and targets.

Flashforwards meet the clients where they are, then advance the sale rapidly toward a win for the client and for you. The goal is to give the client confidence that the journey is worth it and doable, so they engage with you in the process of co-creating their ideal solution.

Give the future-facing version of Why, What, Why a try. Create a flashforward for a client you are currently working with. Practice sharing it with a colleague, then ask for feedback. Did it take less than three to four minutes to share? Did you end by soliciting a response from your colleague? Was it relevant, distinct, and memorable?

As you've seen in this chapter, you must go beyond boilerplate answers and frame your past experiences and future results in terms of the client's specific needs, using a concise Why, What, Why framework. In the next chapter, we'll apply that same framework to one of the most common questions in sales: How are you different?

KEY INSIGHTS FOR SKILL 3

- Use flashback stories to vividly and succinctly show how a similar client's outcomes were both different and better than what they were previously doing, thanks to your experience partnering on a solution.
  - Flashback stories build credibility and confidence in you, your organization, and your team's capacity to provide the correct solution. They help the client conclude they could experience a successful outcome as well.
  - Use the Why, What, Why format when presenting a flashback story:
    - *Why* did the former client need help?
    - *What* did they do, achieve, and learn as a result?
    - *Why* does this story matter to your current client?

- Use flashforward stories to paint an exciting vision of future events as well as the critical milestones in the journey to get there.
  - Flashforward stories build drama and intrigue by showing the difference between what is (the current state as described in the first why) and what could be (the desired future state as portrayed in the second why). These stories help the client build confidence in your ability to take the journey with them and co-create their desired solution.
  - Use the Why, What, Why format as your flashforward story structure. This will keep your story concise and focused, and allow you to customize it for different clients and their unique needs.
  - Flashforward stories are brief and simple in early-stage sales meetings. In middle to late-stage meetings, the flashforward changes from a high-level story to an iterative process where you and the client work together to co-create a solution that exactly meets their needs.

Skill 4: BECOME ESSENTIAL WITH WHY US! DIFFERENTIATORS

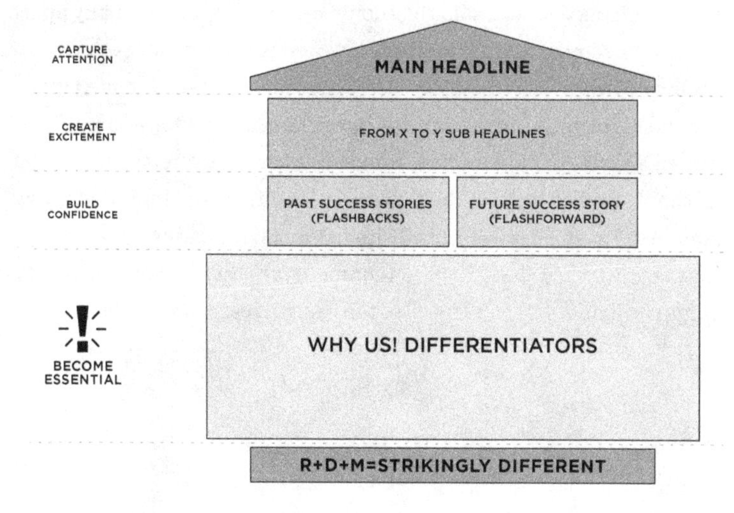

Can your clients tell the difference between you and your competitors? Or do you all look and sound the same? Here's the thing. Clients make decisions based on *differences,* not similarities. So your differences must *stand out.*

As a profession, we're struggling to differentiate. Recall that in our research with Primary Intelligence, buyers saw no difference between vendors 42 percent of the time.

To demonstrate this problem, we conducted an informal experiment (and yes, you can try this at home). We visited the websites of five top professional services companies and compared their content and messages. We tried swapping the name and logo from one company's website to another and guess what—we couldn't tell them apart.

There's more bad news. The truth is, we can't even tell ourselves apart. We recently coached a group of twenty-four senior executives at a consulting company in a *Strikingly Different* work session. They worked in the public sector (i.e., government services) part of the business. We got a lot of pushback from several of the executives when we shared the results of our informal differentiation experiment described above. Several of the executives said they didn't believe us. In fact, as a group, they challenged us and said they could easily tell their company apart from their competitors—especially if we focused on content relevant to their world of government services. We accepted the challenge. On the second morning we were together, we selected three top competitors, pulled a key value statement from the government services section of their respective websites, removed their logos, included a key statement from our client's website in the mix, and asked the twenty-four executives to identify which company was theirs. Here are the key value statements we presented to the executives.

Which statement is from your company's website?

Company 1

Every day, our employees come to work with one focus: our customers' missions. Whether it's protecting citizens or advancing the boundaries of science, these missions are some of the most important and challenging in the world. We bring an unwavering commitment to help our customers succeed, and it's that sense of purpose and opportunity to make a difference in the world that drives us every day.

Helping the future arrive is what we do. We solve the great problems of our times. We create the innovative technologies that define eras. While no one knows what's going to change the world next, we're probably already working on it.

Company 2

We believe that great outcomes are everything. It's what drives us to turn bold ideas into breakthrough solutions. By combining digital technologies with what works across the world's leading businesses, we use agile approaches to help clients solve their toughest problems fast—the first time. So you can deliver what matters most.

Count on us to help you embrace new ways of working, building for change, and putting customers at the core. We bring over 30 years of experience serving the federal government, including every cabinet-level department. Our dedicated colleagues and change makers work with our clients at the heart of the nation's priorities in defense, intel, public safety, health, and civilian to help you make a difference for the people you employ, serve, and protect.

Company 3

Whether ensuring the safety, security, and well-being of citizens or boosting national competitiveness, we work with leaders in civil government to support their public service missions.

We excel at tackling the most complex challenges, from improving information sharing among law enforcement organizations and supporting green initiatives.

Our work spans the full breadth of civil government, including energy and the environment, financial services, health, homeland security, law enforcement, transportation, grants, international development and diplomacy, and benefits and entitlements.

Company 4

We believe our people, ideas, technology, and outcomes are all designed for impact. We bring fresh perspective—from inside and outside government—to help solve our nation's biggest challenges. From cyber and IT modernization to big data and analytics, cloud, anti-fraud, and leadership services, we bring insights from our client experience and research to our consulting and advisory services—to drive bold and lasting results.

Our fresh ideas and insights, along with our shared purpose and passion, help government achieve its mission in innovative new ways. You can make an impact that matters. We work with our government clients to look deeper and find a path forward to deliver meaningful, lasting results.

So how did they do? Fifteen out of twenty-four of the executives failed and picked a competitor's information as their own. It's an understatement to say they were individually and collectively surprised.

All along the sales cycle, from initiation to co-creating a solution, to the final presentation, clients are going to ask, "So how are you different?" Even if they don't ask the question out loud, they are always thinking it.

Let's review a quick example of what typically happens when salespeople answer that question, based on a composite of the hundreds of interactions we witnessed in the sales simulations. In this example, a salesperson has turned in a final proposal and is now getting feedback from the client. As you read this, evaluate what elements you commonly see or hear in your meetings.

Client: I've read through your proposal; I understand the numbers. What I'd really like to learn today is why. Why should we choose you? What do you offer us that your competitors can't?

Salesperson: Thank you for meeting with me. I'm glad you read the proposal, and I'm very excited to be here with you today. Our biggest difference that I'd mention is we are the number-one global company in data analytics. As you probably noticed in our proposal, our consultants have extensive experience. We take care of all your data analytics needs so you can focus on running your core business. Just to give you an idea about our clientele, on my trip here this morning, I passed five headquarters of companies that we represent already, and there's a couple who we're pitching right now. So I hope that gives you some comfort, as far as what we can deliver for you.

DEBRIEF

Salesperson: I liked our opening; I thought it went well. We hit the major points. Even if it was a little bit redundant, it's good to reinforce those points.

Client: It didn't move me. The opening statement was the same message I've been hearing from everyone.

Client: I get that, and it is an impressive clientele. I don't know that we're exactly the same as some of those clients. But let me tell you this: when I first received your proposal, I immediately went to the last page because I knew the price would be there. I'm mentioning that so you understand how important that is to me.

Salesperson: Sure.

Client: And $700,000, I can tell you now, is a deal breaker. I have a budget of $500,000. If you can give me exactly what we need, I could increase that a little bit, by five to ten percent, but you have to understand that $700,000 is out of the question. Can you work within my budget?

Salesperson: We will do everything that we possibly can to get that number as low as possible, where there's a great balance between the value that we provide and the cost we can get for you. But I do want to point out that there's a lot of value built into that price that translates directly to your customer. I think you would find within a year you would exponentially pay back that investment.

Client: I'm aware of that, and I understand return on investment. I'm just going to ask you flat out: can you do this for $500,000?

DEBRIEF

Salesperson: The client caught me off guard a little bit, but at the same time, I was thinking, "Let's just make it through to the next round."

When the salesperson was asked, "How are you different?" they answered with their position in the industry—they never connected the dots on how that would matter to the client in front of them beyond "This should give you comfort." (Notice that the client was *not* comforted by that statement.) The conversation then slipped out of the salesperson's control soon after and devolved into a conversation on price.

When a seller recites generic company differences, without relating to the customer's specific situation and needs, the differences look inconsequential. And the smaller the contrasts are, the more likely a customer is to say, "I don't see a difference here. Vendors one, two, and three look the same. So I'll just buy on price."

Let's try this with your organization. How do you currently answer the question, "What makes your company different?"

____

____

____

____

Over the six years we spent doing our research, we asked the clients what they needed and wanted to hear when the seller was sharing their differences. The clients said sellers make it too hard to determine how they're different in two key ways:

1. **Seller differences are too focused on themselves, their solution, and their company.** Now clearly, at some point you need to mention your experience, tools, technology, and people. But if it feels focused on you and who you are, as opposed to how those differences are going to help the client, you're going to lose their interest. The key is proportion.
2. **Sellers are often unable to show how their differences would create a competitive advantage for the client.** Remember it's not enough to be different, or even dramatically different. Although clients make decisions based on differences, *the client must value those differences.*

BECOMING RELEVANT, DISTINCT, AND MEMORABLE

Let's remember what it means to become Strikingly Different with the simple formula we've been discussing:

RELEVANT + DISTINCT + MEMORABLE (RDM) = STRIKINGLY DIFFERENT

Relevant: Focus on what matters most to the client.

Distinct: Show something that is different and better.

Memorable: Make it "sticky": easy to share and hard to forget.

Think about those two challenges that we just shared: the differences are too focused on the seller, and they can't translate those differences to a competitive advantage for the client. What is missing?

- **Relevant:** Frame your differences in terms of the client's issues, goals, drivers, circumstances, desired outcomes, and emotions.
- **Distinct:** Admittedly, it's tough to stand apart when you may have similar technology, years of experience, processes, and so forth, compared to your competitors. You can start to stand out by sharing From–To statements and showing the client how you're going to help *them* be distinct in their market.
- **Memorable:** Much like in a flashback and flashforward, delivering the differentiators in a simple Why, What, Why framework will make them sticky—easy to share and hard to forget. Going a step further, the differentiators will become *easy to repeat,* meaning the client can restate the differentiators to other stakeholders to gain internal buy-in.

THE WHY US! DIFFERENTIATION FRAMEWORK

When a client asks *how you are different,* instead of blurting out generic, lofty marketing platitudes, let's use something that actually works—the Why Us! differentiation framework. The framework uses the same Why, What, Why pattern as flashbacks and flashforwards, just applied to standing out in a different way. In short, we want to share a key differentiator contrasted with a point of comparison, what we will do with that difference for the client, and why the difference matters to the client, followed by a question: "Do you believe we're different?"

Why Us! Differentiation Framework

WHY US! Differentiators	Include a point of comparison for each difference.
WHAT we will do	For each difference, briefly describe a unique aspect of what you do that will make a real difference to the client.
WHY our differences matter	Explain why each difference will help the client achieve different and better outcomes.

▼

Do you believe we are different?

Often, just one main differentiator, shared using the Why, What, Why pattern described above, will be enough to stand out as different and better to the client. If you can come up with one or two additional differentiators, that's even more impactful.

Here's an important tip on the best way to share up to three differences in a way that sounds conversational. Start with a quick transition statement and an overall headline of all three differentiators. Then go back to your first differentiator and share the point of comparison, what you will do, and why that difference matters to the client. Then do the same with your second differentiator, and finally your third. See example dialogue on the following pages.

Remember that with flashbacks, one of the mistakes salespeople made most in our simulations was that they would share a past success story, feel really pumped about it, then forget to ask the client to react. When sharing differentiators, we want to ask an open-ended question so we can uncover where the client still sees gaps. That's the beauty of this structure: it positions differentiators in the ways *the client* likes to talk about them, so they can then give us feedback and we can figure out what needs to change.

Let's share an example of Why Us! differentiation based on real-world experience in healthcare. You are preparing to meet with Sasha, a senior executive from a large healthcare system that operates numerous hospitals, skilled nursing facilities (SNF), and a home healthcare service in multiple locations. They have been dealing with skyrocketing member costs, increasing lengths of stay at their SNFs, and negative social media trends. You talked with one of Sasha's direct reports, and they told you everyone is feeling a lot of frustration and the team is at the breaking point. You prepare three differentiators using the Why Us! Differentiation Framework:

Why Us! Healthcare Client Example

	DIFFERENTIATOR 1	DIFFERENTIATOR 2	DIFFERENTIATOR 3
WHY US!	**Lower Risk** Our team has implemented five similar engagements and will avoid the trouble spots versus figuring it out as we go.	**Start Big and Zoom Small** We do macro and micro analytics versus siloed work on individual facilities.	**We Get Social!** We bring social media experts as part of your core team instead of just having them available.
WHAT we will do	We will leverage our relevant learnings and bring a clear view of what works and what doesn't work to your operation. This will enable us to drive the great results you're looking for while reducing the risk of implementation.	We will deploy our proprietary health analytics platform across your entire system and then zoom in on specific facilities.	We know this is an important need for you. Our social media team will analyze ongoing trends using a 3-step process. Then, together with your team, they will recommend appropriate actions that will allow you to quickly address negative trends and turn them around.
WHY our difference matters	Our team will help you LOWER member costs by up to 11% AND realize BETTER health outcomes at the same time.	Our platform will help you diagnose, then prescribe which units to focus on first, driving the best outcomes in the shortest amount of time.	Our social media experts will help you go from negative social media trends to positive trending within four months.

Do you believe we are different?

Here's how the seller would share the differentiators when the client asks, "How are you different?" during the client meeting.

Transition and Overall Headline

SURPRISINGLY AVERAGE	STRIKINGLY DIFFERENT
Well, we are very different from our competitors.	Our clients tell us there are several things that make us noticeably different. As it relates to your specific challenges, three things come to mind that I believe will help you close the performance gaps you've been describing and achieve different and better outcomes: we're lower risk, we start big and zoom small, and we get social. Let me give you one cut deeper on each of these.

Differentiator 1

SURPRISINGLY AVERAGE	STRIKINGLY DIFFERENT
First, and probably most important, we have deep healthcare experience. We've been working in this industry for more than a decade.	**Why Us!** First, we're lower risk. We've implemented five similar engagements over the past eighteen months and will avoid the trouble spots instead of figuring it out as we go. **What we will do** We'll bring the team that solved similar challenges with other healthcare systems and bring a clear view of what works and what doesn't work to your operation. This will enable us to drive the great results you're looking for while reducing the risk of implementation. **Why our difference matters** Our team will help you LOWER member costs by up to 11% AND realize BETTER health outcomes at the same time.

Differentiator 2

SURPRISINGLY AVERAGE	STRIKINGLY DIFFERENT
Second, we have a proprietary health analytics platform. It is state of the art and crunches numbers like no other platform I've seen.	**Why Us!** Number two, we start big and zoom small. That means we do macro and micro analytics versus siloed work on individual facilities in your system. **What we will do** We'll deploy our proprietary health analytics platform across your entire system and then zoom in on specific facilities. **Why our difference matters** Our platform will help you diagnose, then prescribe which units to focus on first, driving the best outcomes in the shortest amount of time.

Differentiator 3

SURPRISINGLY AVERAGE	STRIKINGLY DIFFERENT
Third, we have a lot of social media experience that could help you.	**Why Us!** And finally, we get social. We understand how important it is. It's a vital part of doing business today. Our social media experts will be an integral part of the engagement instead of just having them available. **What we will do** Our social media team will analyze ongoing trends using a 3-step process. Then, together with your team, they will recommend appropriate actions that will allow you to quickly address negative trends and turn them around. **Why our difference matters** This will help you turn social media into a positive force instead of a negative drag while transferring know-how to your team. **Ask the question** So as you've heard us share those differences, do you believe we're different?

The Strikingly Different way of sharing the differences isn't, "Hey, we've got cool technology," or "We've got bright team members and social media experts." The difference between a Surprisingly Average and a Strikingly Different approach is showing contrast and relating our differences directly to the client's most important drivers, goals, challenges, and obstacles. Can you see some of the emotion we reference in the above example? Some of the frustration?

Compare this to the "I passed five of our clients' offices on the way here" example. If that seller had used Why Us! differentiators, they would have had a higher likelihood of connecting in the short time they had with that client and helping the client to appreciate not just the return on investment, but what that means for the emotions and symptoms associated with their challenges.

PREPARING YOUR WHY US! DIFFERENTIATORS

When you're preparing a differentiation framework for an early-stage interaction, start by thinking through the client's top issues, goals, drivers, or challenges. Then review what you have achieved (or your organization has achieved) for others. Do you have key differentiators and points of comparison that are relevant for your prospective client? What will you do with those differences to help this particular client? Finally, thinking about why your differences matter, do you have results that are conservative and reasonable enough to use with this client? If not, could you use a range like "eight to ten percent"?

If you truly don't have numbers you can share, just remove them and make the statement more of a summation of what you've seen from others in the marketplace: "In most cases, our team can help you lower member costs and realize better health outcomes at the same time." That paradox itself automatically should get you some dialogue back and forth, and maybe even give them a reason to share their numbers with you.

You can even spin this a different way. If you're trying to say why your difference matters in deep healthcare experience and proprietary health analytics platform, you could ad lib a bit and say something like, "Probably all of our competitors will tell you they can lower member costs. But it is highly unusual to lower member costs and get better health outcomes at the same time. The reason we feel so confident saying that is because our experienced team has done this so many times. And we do something that is highly unusual in the market on the healthcare analytics platform. Most of our competitors have great people who are highly intelligent, and they might even have some good experience. But oftentimes they're guessing exactly how to help you. The big benefit of this platform is you're not going to be guessing. You can actually diagnose and prescribe exactly what you need, nothing more, nothing less. That's pretty different, and I don't know anybody who brings the social media experience along with that."

If a client does challenge you on one of your differentiators (which we hope they would because that would make for fabulous conversation), you can say, "We're in the early stage of working together, but the reason we're saying you could get these kinds of results is because we're seeing them with the other healthcare systems we're working with. And our experience tells us it is highly likely we can help you achieve similar results."

Exercise: Draft Your Why Us! Differentiators

Using the prompts below, try creating a few differentiators for an upcoming client interaction.

What do you think are this client's top issues, goals, drivers, or challenges?

___

___

___

___

What are your organization's two or three big differences that you think are going to matter the most to them?

Briefly, what would your organization do?

Why would those differences matter to your client?

Assess your draft statements using RDM as your filter, then practice delivering them out loud in under sixty seconds per differentiator. Seek out a colleague to give you feedback. Have them play the role of the client and simply ask you, "Why your company?" Respond using the framework, beginning with a transition statement.

Remember: We're not looking for perfection here. We're looking for something real, authentic, and natural. We're aiming for RDM, but our differences may still be a bit fuzzy to the client even after we think we've shared them clearly and concisely. Just like our movie trailers, flashbacks, and flashforwards, it's the *dialogue* that comes from this that we want. Do those differences matter to the client? Is there something we're missing? Maybe they'd come back and say, "It's really going to come down to speed and risk for us." If that's the case, we'd want to move off our prepared differentiators and talk about it: "Tell me more about this. Why are speed and risk the most important to you? What are the reasons you bring that up?" That same iterative process works within the client's organization moving through the sales cycle.

In Part 1, we've built a message house that contains our key messages under one "roof," each tested through the RDM lens. The purpose of the message house is not to showcase our prospecting skills or industry knowledge, but to put intriguing ideas on the table for the client to respond to—ideas around how *they* can achieve remarkable results.

As we head into Part 2, remember that validating and co-creating is the whole game—refining and fine-tuning our messaging and ideas to exactly what the client needs, *in their opinion*. We partner together to help clients realize different and better outcomes. When our story becomes their story, we're on the way to winning the business.

KEY INSIGHTS FOR SKILL 4

- Remember to use the Why, What, Why pattern when sharing your key differentiators.
- Always include a point of comparison for each differentiator, otherwise it will not sound unique or will sound like everyone else. Stay away from things that everyone can claim (e.g., "Our people work hard" or "We're committed to your success").
- Connect the dots for the client. They won't do it on their own. Explain why your differences will help the client achieve different and better outcomes (e.g., "Our differences and what we do with them will increase speed, decrease cost, lower risk, ease your workload, enable good decisions, etc.").

PART 2
VALIDATE & CO-CREATE

Skill 5: GET CURIOUS AND FIND THE GAPS

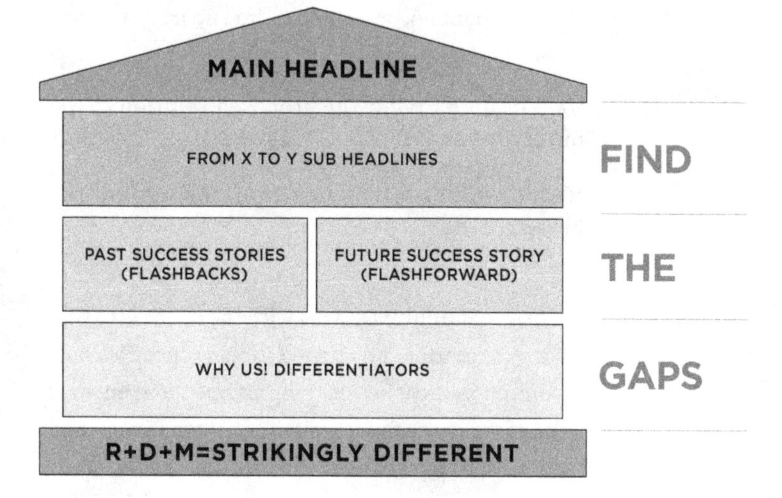

After spending so much time and effort perfecting our billboards, movie trailers, flashbacks, flashforwards, and Why Us! differentiators, we might be tempted to just center the conversation around these messages. But the point of each of those story forms is to put forward something the client can respond to, beginning a back-and-forth dialogue between the seller and the client.

Unfortunately, many salespeople believe that if they talk enough, they can convince the client to buy. That paradigm cuts short the critical discovery dialogue that identifies the client's real issues and motivators.

Our research with Primary Intelligence found some troubling statistics about salespeople's ability to understand clients' needs:

- The number one cited sales issue that needed to be addressed to win was understanding buyer needs.
- Understanding buyer needs was the single most important sales criteria to buyers by a factor of three (i.e., it's three times more important than the next most important sales criteria, which were responsiveness and product knowledge).
- As deal size increases, the ability of the sales team to understand buyer needs *diminishes*.
- The top three root causes for failing to understand the buyer's needs were:
    - Vendor spent no, or too little, time up front to learn about the buyer.
    - Vendor didn't tailor the proposed solution to the buyer's needs.
    - Vendor didn't tailor presentations around the buyer's needs.

Remember our goal in sharing our messages with the client is to find out if the messages are insightful and aligned to their specific goals and issues. If not, where are the gaps? Having an open and curious mindset will assist us as we check for relevancy, distinctiveness, and memorability. It will signal to our client that we are open to their feedback as they react and even disagree with us. This essential feedback will often change our assumptions and the content of the messages. We need to find out directly from the client if we've gotten their themes, circumstances, emotions, and outcomes right in our messages. For our message house to eventually become their house, it needs the client's active involvement that can only come as we co-create these essential messages together.

To validate and co-create, we do something we call "move off the message house and its related solutions." To "move off" means that after sharing our billboard, movie trailer, or any other message or experience, we ask an open-ended question to find out if we are focused on the right goals, challenges, and drivers of our client.

If we don't move off the message house and its related solutions, or if we do it poorly, we'll likely spend most of our initial client dialogue talking about our messages. The clients will ask *us* questions. We will do all the work, and by the end of the conversation, we will have little understanding, and no validation, of what's important to the client.

Here's the thing: There is no inherent value in the message house. There's *potential* value, but there's no actual value until we validate and co-create it with the client. The message house and its related solutions only create value when they solve problems that clients have or create results they want.

We're starting with potential value, what we think would work, but no matter how much preparation we do, we may be off. That message house and all the messages inside need to shift so we can get more and more RDM and help clients see how working together will make them (the client) different and better.

As salespeople, we shouldn't be androids who are so slick that the message gets lost. We should be authentic and human and vulnerable—willing to listen. The best salespeople are humble enough to put forward good thought leadership and still realize that it has no inherent value, so they need to quickly move off it, listen to the client, and focus on what will help *the client* succeed. What business issues do they have and what do they want to achieve? Are we in alignment with these things? Then we focus our experience, messages, and related solutions on what matters most to the client so that the message house becomes *their* message house.

MOVE OFF THE MESSAGE HOUSE

Let's walk through how you can get curious and find the gaps in the message house. Finding the gaps means understanding the client's business problem and desired results and refining, adapting, and co-creating the message house to be spot-on with what the client needs.

The skill set "move off the message house/solution" helps us to move the conversation away from us and our needs toward what is important for the client. The goal is to have the client start talking about the problems or results they're hoping the message house and related solutions will address. Ultimately, our sincere listening will unlock an exchange of information. That is the way to balance advocacy—our ideas—with inquiry in a client-focused way.

For simplicity in the following illustration and discussion, we'll refer to the message house and its related solutions collectively as the "solution."

Imagine you share a movie trailer with a client, and when you ask, "What are your thoughts?" they either 1) ask you a question about how you would go about delivering on one of the From–To outcomes you just mentioned or 2) make a statement about some aspect of what you just shared. To handle either scenario, let's go over a simple process for moving off the solution. There are three parts:

"Move Off the Solution" Formula

Move to Business Problems
OR
Move to Business Results

First, listen carefully to what the client asks or says.

Second, use a softening and/or clarifying statement. The **softening statement** is a transition from the clients' question or statement to your response so you create an open, honest dialogue where the client feels safe to share and explore what they think, feel, and believe to be true. **Clarifying statements** ensure that we aren't guessing about what the client is asking or saying.

Third, ask a "move off the solution" question to shift the conversation from you talking about your solution toward mutual exploration of the business problems the client is trying to solve or the business results they need to achieve. Remember, we want the focus to be on the client.

Here's a quick example of how to flow these three steps into a conversation. In this example, the salesperson shares a billboard focused on how digital automation and artificial intelligence (AI) could help the client gain better insight and enable rapid growth. We'll pick up the conversation with the client's response to the billboard.

Client: Thanks for sharing your perspective. I'm intrigued with your point of view on how digital automation and AI can bring us better insights to drive growth. Let me give you some more color on what's going on with us right now. Like most companies, we definitely need automation to help lower costs and bring new levels of consistency, speed, and scalability to our business processes. But to be disruptive, we have to unleash the ingenuity of our people. I think AI could give us the edge we need. Tell us more about your experience in AI.

[1. Listen carefully to what the client asks you.]

Salesperson: I'd be happy to. To get you that edge, we believe the way you go about implementing AI is really important.

[2. Use a softening statement]

Salesperson: Before I get into all of that, let me just pause for a minute and ask a couple questions so I can give you my best thinking.

[3. Ask a "Move Off the Solution" question.]

Salesperson: Let's say you did unleash the ingenuity of your people. What specific business results are you hoping that you will drive?

Client: Interesting question. I would say...

WHAT CLIENTS WANT

Clients want us to truly listen with the intent to understand. It sounds simple, and yet most of us find this incredibly difficult in practice. Recently, we interviewed executives from tech, banking, real estate, and other industries about how they like to be sold to and what absolutely drives them crazy. One error was so common that executives called it the "Hall of Fame crash-and-burn": not listening. Here are direct quotes from the executives we interviewed about how salespeople get this essential skill wrong:

- "[Executives] like to talk about their business if you give them the chance. **You'll find out a lot...if you just stop talking.** It amazes me that this is still the biggest single issue salespeople have. They don't listen. They're too anxious to tell their story. They've been trained to tell their story, and they're going to tell that story whether you want them to or not."
- **"If you don't bring anything to the second meeting that reflects the information you learned in the first meeting, it will end really fast.** That information is an advantage a salesperson has over the competition. A lot of times, those differences between competitors are not that clear. In fact, they're pretty much the same. So at the end of the day, it's going to come down to buying that person, that team, that company. **I'm buying them because they listened.** I believe it's in their culture; therefore, when I get to the project, I'm going to have people there who are going to listen to my people. It says that listening is probably important internally. It's probably a skill that the company is working on: that in meetings, they listen

to each other and take from that value and translate that value into action."

- "I've literally had people come into my office and ask me an initial leading question and follow that up with a monologue. They ask me one question, I start to answer, they interrupt and then launch into a story that revolves around everything they've ever done, everything the product does, everything their service provides, how they can help when they get started. It's too much, too soon."
- "The body gives off a tremendous amount of information if you just bother to observe it. Frequently salespeople come in with their PowerPoint, and they're going to get through it regardless of anything else. And the person you're talking to will tell you either verbally or nonverbally, 'Please don't do this to me.'"
- "Salespeople listen so rarely that I found myself doing a whole lot of coaching. Like stopping them and saying, 'Listen, I'm going to tell you exactly what we need.' They still don't listen, even when they're being told exactly what the client needs."
- "Talking too much is clearly a sign of insecurity, that you are uncomfortable engaging in one-on-one dialogue. You feel like you need to fill up the empty space with words, and the conversation becomes a meaningless word salad. **Listening is a good skill in terms of the selling interaction, because people will eventually tell you what you want to know.** They may not tell you as fast as you want to know it. They may not tell you in a logical order, but people will eventually tell you what you want to know if you just listen long enough."

The executives in our sales simulations echoed this feedback. They loved to have salespeople come and share their thoughts and experience. But across the globe, in many different organizations and companies, executives said the same thing: "Take two or three minutes to put the idea on the table, then engage me. Let me weigh in on your initial thoughts, ask a few high-level questions, or provide a little more context." In other words, clients are saying: "Keep me involved, let's have a dialogue and explore together." So, listen and clarify and connect with the client. Earn the right to ask more questions about the business challenges they need to solve or the business results they would like to achieve. Dialogue, not monologue, is how you find the gaps in the message house and discover how to close them in the client's best interest.

Here are some tips for asking effective questions and for effective listening.

HINTS FOR ASKING EFFECTIVE QUESTIONS	HINTS FOR EFFECTIVE LISTENING
• Ask for permission to ask questions. • Ask one question at a time; wait for the answer. • Reward their response, then ask your next question. (When appropriate, use their words from their questions: it's a powerful reward.) • Be cautious of leading questions (questions designed to get agreement, not information or understanding).	• Listening is a matter of choice and concentration. **Choice:** You must choose to listen actively. **Concentration:** Focus your complete attention on the other person. • Focus on the client's answer, not on your next question. • Be aware of and lower your internal dialogue. • Listen with your ears, watch with your eyes, sense with your intuition the real meaning of the client's communication. Is there a difference between what they said and what they meant?

SEVERAL GREAT CHOICES

Let's look at another example. Suppose that we're talking with a client and they ask us what experience we have helping companies similar to theirs. In response, we share a flashback and the client says, "I really like what you did with that other company. Our situation is similar, but with a couple of important differences. I think the way I would sum it up is we need a platform to harness business-critical information. That way we can make faster, smarter, strategic decisions without a huge investment of time or money. And I'm wondering, is that where you're headed? Can you help us in this area?"

We have several choices here, particularly when we look at that second step around softening and clarifying. One approach is to **soften and clarify:** "Yes, I'm glad you said something. There are several ways we might be able to help. So I can give you my best thinking, what information is business critical to you?" Don't assume; slow down and clarify the particularly meaningful statement that they shared.

Here's another option: **soften and move to a technical discussion.** The client in this example mentioned a platform. So we might say, "I would imagine that we can. Help me to understand a little more, what platform are you currently using?"

Or we might need additional clarification on something the client said. But whether we need that clarification or not, the ultimate goal is to move to either understanding the problems they have or the results they need.

Finally, we might **soften and move to business outcomes:** "I believe there may be several ways we can help you make faster, smarter, better decisions. Before I respond, tell me: what are some of the business problems or challenges that you would like to address with this new platform?" Or you might say, "Let's explore this together. I'm curious—if you could make faster, smarter strategic decisions, what key business results would you expect to achieve?"

"Move Off the Solution" Best Practices

Use the Client's Exact Words and Phrases:

- Your version of those words may not resonate with the client.
- You avoid confusing the dialogue with a translated version of their words.
- You demonstrate your ability to listen and understand their perspectives first.

Avoid Using "But":

- "But" tends to erase everything that comes before it. See if you can just end the sentence, or use "and."
    - For example: "That's an intriguing perspective and it would be great if you could help me understand..."

Sometimes it's a challenge determining if you should move to problems or to results. How do you decide which way to go? It depends on the language. If a client is saying, "We're struggling, we're having challenges in this area. We need to move away from this or make this critical move," in many cases they're wanting to talk about the current state. So, move toward the problems. And then the opposite is also true. If they say, "We need to achieve X, we're looking out into the future, here's the strategy we're trying to accomplish," that might be a natural time to say, "Let's look at that. If you could get that result, what would that allow you to do as a business that you're not able to do today?" Or, you could say, "Imagine you achieve X in the best way possible. What key business results would you expect to see?"

The skill of moving off the message house/solution creates the environment and demonstrates the intent that we are interested in and paying attention to what the client says, and it matters to us. We're moving *off* our message house/solution to learn from the client, so we can eventually move back *on* to the message house and refine the messages in anticipation of a final proposal or presentation. It becomes a virtuous cycle of getting closer and closer to what the client wants, and in the process, we stand out as being Strikingly Different.

STRUCTURE THE CONVERSATION

As we invite our clients to move off the message house/solution, there are times when we need to further deepen our understanding of the problems the client needs to solve or the results they want to generate.

We met Sophia, a UK-based salesperson, in London at a work session we were conducting. She worked for a large software company and told us she was having a hard time getting her customers to open up and share meaningful information about their business issues. We taught her how to move off the solution and structure a conversation, then coached her on several ways she could deepen and broaden her conversations. A month later, we got back together with Sophia to give her some more coaching. As soon as we saw her, she excitedly said, "I just had an amazing experience with moving off the solution and structuring a conversation. I was talking with the CIO of a distribution company about a security problem they were having. The solution they wanted was pretty small—about £50,000. I told the CIO we could absolutely help. Then, I got curious and interested and said, 'Could we just talk for a few minutes so I can understand a bit more about what's going on right now in your organization, and then I'll give you my best thinking on how you might solve your security issue?' " And then Sophie moved off the solution and structured a conversation. Sophie told us, "When I summarized the conversation back to the CIO, I realized that what they needed, and what we could help them with, was much bigger than the solution I had in mind. The customer went from a £50,000 security solution to a £1,300,000 implementation of software and processes that will upgrade and absolutely move their company forward in a major way."

Structuring the conversation is a highly effective approach to conduct an enjoyable and rewarding in-depth dialogue with clients. As Sophie discovered, it helps us to be client centric even with a solution-centered client.

There are five steps to structure the conversation with a client:

1. Get a quick list of all the issues (problems and results).
2. Make sure the list of issues is complete.
3. Find out which issue is most important to the client.
4. Go into depth—develop evidence and impact on the priority issue.
5. Summarize everything you've heard by asking, "Did I get it right? Did I leave anything out?"

Let's walk through a few definitions.

- **Issues** are problems to be solved or results to be achieved.
- **Evidence** answers the question, "What are you seeing, hearing, or feeling that lets you know this is an issue?" Evidence is a description of how an issue shows up in an organization. Some questions you would ask around evidence would be "How specifically does that issue you mentioned show up?" or "What two or three key metrics need to change as it relates to that particular issue?" or "What lets you know this is a problem?" or "How will you measure success?"
- **Impact** is how the issue affects the business. It answers the question, "What makes this issue important to you?" or, more bluntly, "So what and who cares?" Impact can be quantitative (a financial consequence) or qualitative (reputation, image, political, personal consequence). Some questions you could ask around impact would be "Worst case scenario, let's say you don't solve the problem or achieve the results we're discussing—then what happens?" or "Best-case scenario, let's say you do accomplish what you set out to do; what would that allow you to do that you can't do today?"

Let's do a quick run-through of the steps of the conversation and point out a few best practices.

5 Easy Steps to Structure the Conversation

1. Get a quick list of all the issues.
2. Make sure the list is complete.
3. Find out which issue is most important to the client.
4. Go into depth—develop evidence and impact.
5. Summarize:
   - Did I get it right?
   - Did I leave anything out?

First, get a quick list of all the issues, defined as problems to be solved or results to be achieved as it relates to the message you put before them. Notice the word "quick"—you want the top-of-mind things from the client.

Once you've made sure the list is complete by asking if there's anything else they want to add, check for the most important issue. It'll sound something like this: "You've mentioned issues A, B, C, and D. Of all those, which might be most important to you and your situation?" And the client will tell you which one, and you'll go into depth on and develop evidence and impact around that.

Finally, you'll want to summarize the conversation with them: "You've mentioned five issues as very important for you right now, and you said the third one is the most important. You described how it's showing up in your business. We've discussed the impact as to what makes them so important to you. Did I get it right? .... Did I leave anything out?"

"Did I get it right?" is an accuracy question. "Did I leave anything out?" is a completeness question.

This is a very thorough approach to having a conversation, and you can flex it anywhere from ten minutes to thirty minutes to an hour across multiple people in the client organization.

Best Practices

1. *Think of the five steps as a road map.*
    - Even though we show the steps in a linear way, clients will typically move around as they remember things they want to include in the dialogue. A client might give you a priority issue and go directly to the impact on the organization. You will have to circle back to complete the list of issues, then verify the most important issue and check that the evidence really does lead to the impact the client originally stated. Keeping the linear flow of the five steps in mind will help you navigate the conversation.
2. *Get a complete list of issues.*
    - Avoid moving forward in the conversation before capturing all of the issues first.
    - Keep in mind that the first issue mentioned by the client is not always the top-priority issue.
    - Be sure to ask, "Anything else?" two or three times. You may choose to suggest some issues you have seen in the past that the client has not mentioned.
3. *Keep an open mind.*
    - Avoid listening mainly for issues that are familiar to you or for which you have a solution.
    - Invite the client to talk about issues that are important to them—even if they are not within your area of expertise.
4. *Allow the client to determine the top-priority issue.*
    - Keep the focus on what the key motivators are from the perspective of the client.
    - While your own experience and opinions are valuable, be sure you first understand the client's point of view.
5. *Remember the 80/20 rule.*
    - We've found that about 80 percent of the impact is typically in 20 percent of a client's issues. After exploring one or two top issues, you should be able to make some quick

judgments about how big the impact would be relative to the likely investment. When the impact is big, ask the client what has stopped the organization from resolving the issue before this point. When the impact is small, you and/or your client might decide to take away the solution. It's critical to identify this situation early in the sales cycle. Your client will thank you for it, and you will avoid investing time and money in a pursuit that just doesn't warrant it.

Real Estate Example of Structuring the Conversation

For the next few pages, we're going to briefly step away from the B2B business world and use a personal example, then we'll come back and apply what we learned together to a business conversation. While you read, note the five steps of structuring the conversation throughout this example.

Real estate agent: I'm delighted for the call and the opportunity to work with you. I understand you're moving to the area for your job. I'd like to find the perfect home for you, so rather than hopping in the car to look at homes and areas, I'd like to start by asking for a quick list of those things that are important to you as you think about a new home.

[1. Make a quick list of all the issues.]

Buyer: The location of the home needs to be near the top schools, shopping, and good bike trails, because we do a lot of outdoor activities. Since we need to move in quickly, we'd like an existing home built within the last three years. And then, of course, budget is a big deal.

[2. Make sure the list is complete.]

Real estate agent: Anything else?

Buyer: We'd like it to be an open floor plan with the master bedroom on the main level.

Real estate agent: Let's see what we can accomplish. Anything else?

Buyer: No, I think that's it.

[3. Find out which issue is most important.]

Real estate agent: Of the things that you mentioned—location, newer construction, budget, open, master on the main—which of those would you say is the most important?

Buyer: Open, for sure.

Real estate agent: Let's dive a little bit deeper into that to make sure I understand what you're looking for. How would you describe "open"?

Buyer: We need to have a lot of room to gather our family and friends. We want a large kitchen connected to a big, open room; that way, we have plenty of room to gather large groups in one place.

Real estate agent: That makes sense. Anything else?

Buyer: We also want high ceilings and plenty of windows. We like natural light.

Real estate agent: How about the rest of the house?

Buyer: Yes, we want bigger bedrooms with adjoining bathrooms. We often have guests that stay overnight, and we want to have plenty of room for them so they feel comfortable.

Real estate agent: I think I'm starting to get a sense for what you're looking for and what you mean when you say "open." What is it about "open" that makes that so critical for you?

[4. Go into depth.]

Buyer: We are very social people, and for us "home" is about gathering people. For instance, we love to cook. We will often invite a large group of family and friends over to the house. Everyone brings their favorite foods, and we cook together. So, we will need plenty of room in the kitchen along with the adjoining areas. That way, everyone can participate and join in, including any who aren't cooking who are seated nearby. That way we are all together, we can hear each other and be part of the conversation. Being together is what a home is all about.

[5. Summarize.]

Real estate agent: Wow, that sounds like a lot of fun. OK, let me make sure I've gotten an accurate capture of this, and then we'll put together a tour of homes. Let's see, location near schools and outdoor activities, newer construction, has to fit within your budget, and open.

Buyer: Yes.

[5. Summarize—check for accuracy.]

Real estate agent: And of those, the most important is open. And you would describe open as the areas where you spend a lot of time, like in the kitchen and family room, you don't want any separation or walls getting in the way. You want high ceilings and big windows providing lots of natural light. And you want spacious bedrooms with adjoining bathrooms. And the most important thing to remember is your home is a critical place for you to gather and be together with the people you love. So there need to be big, open rooms connected together for you in the main areas so you can cook, gather, and interact. Did I get that right?

Buyer: Yes.

[5. Summarize—check for completion.]

Real estate agent: Anything missing?

Buyer: No, not at all.

Real estate agent: Great, this will allow me to put together a tour of homes that will better meet these needs, so I really appreciate this. It's going to help us both in our search for the perfect home for you.

Buyer: Sounds great. I can't wait to get started.

The five steps helped the seller understand what the buyer was looking for before spending precious time and energy on possible solutions. Structuring the conversation this way deepens your comprehension of what the client means, what they want, and how you can help them.

What did you like about that example? How is this different than what you might normally see? How is this different than what you may have done in the past?

STRUCTURE THE CONVERSATION TO FIND THE GAPS ACROSS THE SALES CYCLE

It's important to remember that the whole reason someone is willing to answer our questions, allow us to move off the solution, and structure the conversation is that they're hoping we're going to give them additional value as a result. And that value usually comes in either a reconfirmation, restatement, or change of the billboard, movie trailer, or flashforward compared to what we started with. Here's how you would do that:

After you reach the Summarize step, particularly in early to mid-stage meetings, the client will often say, "Now that you know something about us and what's going on, what would you do? Where have you done something like this before? Have you helped other clients?" It gives you a beautiful opportunity to share a flashback: "As I've been listening to your issues, evidence, and impact and all you've been dealing with, it caused me to think about an organization we helped just recently. Here's why they needed help, here's what we did, here's what they achieved, and here's why I think that would matter to you." That could be done in the same meeting, or it may need to wait until a second meeting. That's one application of the idea of building confidence around what we've done in the past to help other clients.

Mid-stage in a sales pursuit, we want to co-develop a solution. It's very common for the client to say, "You've spent time with this, and you understand what we're thinking and where we need to go. We'd like to hear what you recommend we do." So we share a flashforward in a Why, What, Why frame and say, "I'm curious: what do *you* see as your ideal solution?" Then repeat the five steps of Structure the Conversation again. Listen to what they're thinking, make the list complete, find out which part of the solution is most important, and get evidence and impact of why the elements of that solution are so important. Perhaps it needs to be onshore/offshore, or maybe it needs to incorporate a certain technology, etc.—find out why they have found that to be so valuable. You're now collaborating and co-creating the message house and solution.

The final application will impact your Why Us! differentiators. We might say, "What are you looking for in the ideal partner?" or "What are you looking for an organization like us to bring? What's going to matter the most to you?" They'll give us a list of that: perhaps experience, expertise in social media, real leadership, governance, a way to reduce risk, etc. We make the list, we make it complete, then we get the most important. Then we go into depth to understand what's *driving* the need for those things and why that matters to them.

As we apply the skills of moving off the solution and structuring the conversation, our message house and related solutions should get better and better throughout the entire sales process—in other words, become more relevant, distinct, and memorable until our message house becomes the client's message house.

In the next chapter, we'll show you how to deal with the inevitable questions, challenges, objections, and concerns you will likely encounter as you move toward closing the sale.

KEY INSIGHTS FOR SKILL 5

- Understanding buyer needs is the single most important sales criteria to buyers by a factor of three.
- Find the gaps in your message house by shifting the conversation from you talking about your message house/solution toward mutual exploration of the business problems the client is trying to solve or the business results they need to achieve.
- Structure the conversation when you need to further deepen your understanding of the problems the client needs to solve or the results they want to generate.

Skill 6: NAVIGATE TRAFFIC LIGHTS AND CLOSE THE GAPS

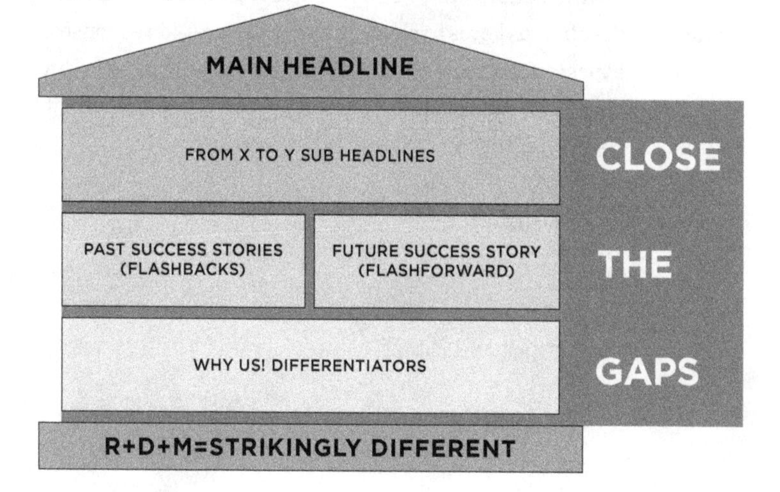

Selling is like driving a car through the city. Some sales pursuits feel like a late-night drive where we mostly encounter intersections with green traffic lights and seldom, if ever, need to slow down for a yellow or stop at a red light. Other pursuits feel much more like a midday drive through city streets, where we see less green and many more yellow and red lights. Then there are those pursuits that feel like the rush-hour grind where we have to slog our way through a constant stream of yellow and red lights to get to our destination.

Whether we are traveling fast or slow, knowing how to successfully navigate the three different colors of traffic lights we encounter in our sales pursuits is vital. In sales, we define **green lights** as client questions and minor concerns we can easily answer and resolve while still moving forward. We define **yellow and red lights** as client pushbacks, challenges, objections, and concerns. It's never a good idea to ignore them, try to go around them, or accelerate through them. Resolving yellow and red lights effectively requires us to slow down or stop, show empathy, and engage in real human-to-human dialogue.

As we validate and co-create our message house together with our client, a natural and normal part of the process is to answer questions and resolve concerns. Some of these questions and situations are predictable, while others come unexpectedly. For those that are predictable, the obvious key is to plan and even practice our responses. But when unexpected concerns arise, you can lean on the framework in this skill to help you find and close the gaps in the message house until it looks like, feels like, and becomes the client's message house.

Let's start with green lights.

GREEN LIGHTS

KEEP MOVING FORWARD.

When a client conversation feels easy, the dialogue seems to flow well, and there is a good exchange of ideas and information, we'd say that's a green light so let's keep moving forward. In these situations, the salesperson and the client work well together toward the common goal of helping the client achieve different and better outcomes. Trust is high, and speed is fast. When questions or minor concerns arise, we simply take our foot off the gas pedal for a moment, listen carefully, answer directly, and explain briefly. As part of the explanation, we might share a billboard, movie trailer, flashback, flashforward, or a Why Us! differentiator. The explanation, along with whatever appropriate story we share, satisfies the client, and we continue moving forward to complete the sale without losing momentum. Sounds perfect, right? We'd love it if every sales pursuit was filled with only green lights. But the reality is that most sales pursuits have several yellow and a few red lights to navigate as we progress the sale.

YELLOW AND RED LIGHTS

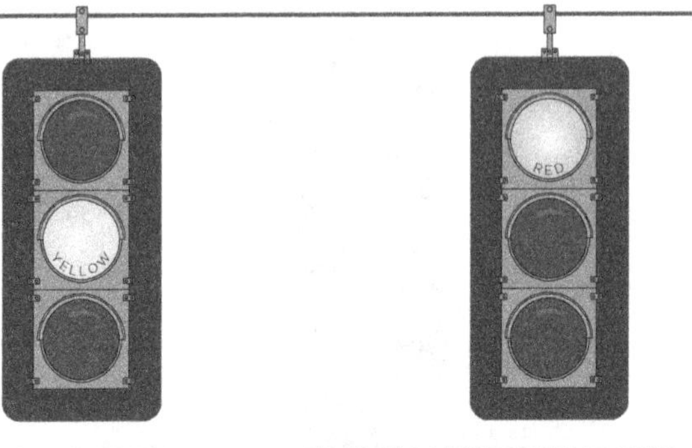

SLOW DOWN. WORK TO TURN THE LIGHT GREEN.

IF THE LIGHT TURNS RED, STOP. WORK TO TURN THE LIGHT GREEN OR EXIT GRACEFULLY.

In sales, navigating yellow lights requires us to slow down. If we resolve the yellow light and it turns green, we step on the gas pedal and accelerate to the appropriate speed to move the sale toward a win. If we can't resolve it, the light turns red. Red lights require us to stop, resolve the concern so the light turns green, or exit the pursuit gracefully.

Acknowledge, Understand, Resolve

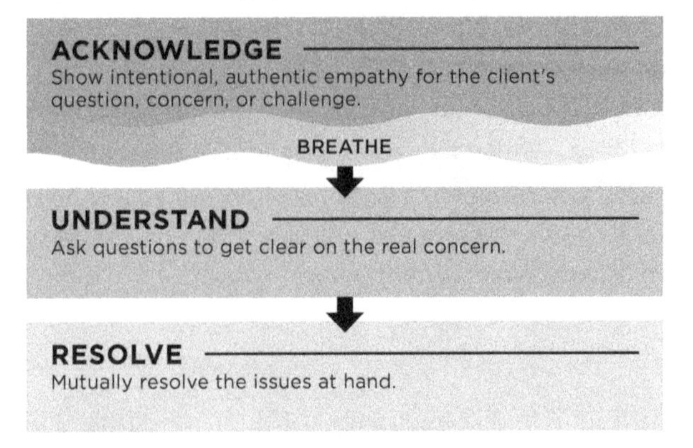

ACKNOWLEDGE, UNDERSTAND, RESOLVE

To navigate yellow and red lights well, we must stay unflappable and apply a dedicated, artful approach. Rarely is it a linear, sequential process. Sometimes we will need all the elements included here and sometimes we won't. Occasionally, we will feel as if we have to start over when we thought we had nearly resolved the client's concerns. This is normal. Be patient and flexible. Effective conflict resolution is extremely satisfying and pays off with uncommon results.

Acknowledge

ACKNOWLEDGE
Show intentional, authentic empathy for the client's question, concern, or challenge.

To acknowledge, show intentional, authentic empathy for the challenge or concern. Empathy can be shown several ways. We can acknowledge the client's concern. We can express appreciation that the client trusts us enough to share their concern. We can share genuine interest in understanding their concern. And we can show our willingness to talk about any concern. Acknowledge is really a skill of emotional intelligence, meaning we're validating, empathizing, confirming, listening, and connecting with the other person. If the client throws a caustic statement at us, we comfortably and confidently absorb the energy and show empathy in return.

We believe that of all the things we share in the pattern to navigate yellow and red lights, empathy is the most important. Because if the client feels like we're on their side, if we authentically validate what they've asked or said, if we convey understanding and demonstrate we've been listening, they will often defuse a very tense situation, making it much easier to resolve the concern. Empathy gives both of us a chance to relax and talk to each other like human beings.

Here's a key point: acknowledging does not mean we agree. This has confused a lot of salespeople, and they make trite statements that do more damage than good like, "I understand," or "I appreciate that," when they clearly don't.

Let's walk through some examples of acknowledging authentically. Imagine that you share something with the client, and they say something like the following:

Client: This simply misses the mark.

Salesperson: Even though that's a big letdown, I'm glad you said something. (pause) May I ask a few questions to make sure I really understand your concerns?

Client: I'm not interested.

Salesperson: Oh, that's not what I expected; thanks for being upfront with me. (pause) May I ask you a few questions to make sure I really understand your concerns?

Notice how the above examples are simple and respectful. We're acknowledging the client without necessarily agreeing. These authentic responses signal to the other person that we care, and we want to know more.

Other examples:

- "Thank you for being straightforward with me."
- "I appreciate you being upfront with me."
- "I'm really sorry to hear that."
- "I definitely hear the concern, and I'm glad you raised it. It would have been easy to gloss over, so let's slow down and talk about it for a minute."

- "I appreciate your honesty. Let's agree that we won't move forward in our discussion until we both feel that we have resolved this in a good, fair way."

Lastly, let's imagine the client asks us a tough question where we need to learn more before answering it. We might say, "That's a tough question. It's a good question, it's just tough to answer. Let's talk it through."

Some objections are difficult to hear, and as a result, hard to acknowledge. Examples include, "I don't like what you're saying," or "I completely disagree," or "I think you're way off the mark." When we hear these types of statements, it's natural for our physical body to react. Our diaphragm will tend to tighten, and we often stop breathing as deeply as we normally do. When we are not breathing normally, we're not receiving as much oxygen to our brain and are not thinking clearly. Have you ever felt that happening during a tough or unexpected challenge? It's hard to interact with a client in a credible and authentic way when we feel too tight. So, between acknowledge and understand, we recommend taking a short break to take a breath. We're not making it overtly obvious, but taking a breath allows us to relax, so we can think clearly, be authentic, and prepare to understand the client's perspective.

Understand

UNDERSTAND
Ask questions to get clear on the real concern.

The second step is to understand—clarifying the real concern so we can work toward a mutual resolution. Rather than moving to understand, salespeople often immediately respond, answer, or defend. They're good problem solvers, so when they hear, sense, or see a challenge, their brains immediately search for an answer. Once they think they have the answer, they jump in. Now if this were a green-light situation, that might be entirely fine, and the answer or solution would likely be accepted. But with a yellow or red light, this approach tends to shut the dialogue down, and we don't ever get to understand clearly what the real concerns are. So resist the urge to solve, respond, or defend. Instead, ask for understanding and perspective.

There are three effective ways to gain better understanding: clarify, reframe, and walk into the future. Each one has its own strengths, and we may not need them all. So, choose wisely and find the right balance. Let's look into each choice.

Understand: Clarify

There are several different ways to clarify. Often the less we say, the better. Key phrases like, "which means?" "such as?" "how so?" "compared to?" and "could you explain that a bit more?" can bring clarity to their point of view and perspective so we can listen and dig deeper.

The bottom-line is this: don't guess what the real issue is. Ask open-ended questions and listen.

If the issue is complex, use the "structure the conversation" framework we shared in Skill 5 to help break down the complexity and better understand their concerns. Remember the five-step structure? 1) Make a list of the issues, 2) make sure it's complete, 3) find out which is most important, 4) go into depth and get evidence and impact, 5) summarize, then ask, "Did I get it right? Did I leave anything out?"

Let's walk through a quick example of how to do this. Suppose the client says, "The business units are not going to buy into this."

- First acknowledge: "Wow, I'm glad you brought that up. If they are not bought in, it wouldn't make sense to move forward. Let me ask you a question. When you say they're not going to buy into this, could you explain specifically what you think they might object to?"
- You can then ask questions to get a quick list of the top concerns.
- Make sure it's complete by asking, "Anything else?"
- Ask, "Of all these concerns, which do you think is the most important?"
- Then go down the path. For example, if they say something like, "You're too expensive." You could say, "Could you clarify—too expensive compared to whom or what?"

Once we clearly understand their concern and have restated it successfully back to them, we can either move on to resolving, or continue to understand a bit more. Beyond clarification, another understanding choice is to reframe.

Understand: Reframe

Have you ever noticed that clients find it easier to tell you all the things they don't like, as opposed to telling you what they *would* like instead?

The concept of reframe, or flip frame, helps the client go from focusing on the negative to focusing on the positive and what they would rather have instead. This is often helpful to do prior to resolving. In some cases, reframing might give us exactly what we need to resolve their concern. It helps us see the gap and how to close it.

Here are several examples of reframing questions we can ask when the client expresses a concern:

- "What would allow you to feel confident and comfortable that this issue will be addressed in a manner that you'll be happy with?"
- "What would you have to see, hear, or experience that would allow you to be confident this issue would be addressed?"
- "What would you have to check off in your mind and your gut before...?"
- "What would have to be in place before...?"
- "How would you become convinced that this would work?"
- "What are the criteria you would need to see addressed in order to...?"

This language reframes the client from the current state, focused on problems, to a future state that would allow them to check off the issue and move forward.

Watch out on this one. It's critical to clearly understand what the concern is and what may not be going well before we ask for the reframe. For instance, if the business units aren't bought in, you might proceed this way:

Salesperson: Are you saying they're not going to buy into the whole project or certain aspects or areas of the project?

Client: Just this aspect.

Salesperson: OK. And they're in sync with the other things we've been discussing?

Client: They are.

Salesperson: Tell me more about the aspect they won't buy into.

[Client explains further.]

Salesperson: I really appreciate understanding more about what they need. I'm not certain we can provide everything they need, but let's suppose we could. What would allow them to feel confident and comfortable that we're meeting their needs? Or what would have to be in place before they would consider this?

Here are a couple more reframing examples.

Client: I'm not confident that you have sufficient experience in our industry niche.

Salesperson: What would you have to see or experience that would cause you to feel confident that we do have sufficient experience?

Client: I need to see probably two case studies in an industry and geography similar to ours.

Salesperson: No problem. Let me share an experience with you. [Share a flashback.]

Client: I've heard your implementation team will come in and steamroll my group with your processes and methodology.

Salesperson: I'm sorry to hear that. That's exactly what we don't want to have happen. [Ask the client to explain experiences they've had in the past or where they heard this so we can understand.] Thanks for sharing that. We certainly don't want to come in and do that, so what would you need to see, hear, or experience to feel comfortable and confident that we wouldn't steamroll your group and you would maintain control?

Note: Remember that we're just homing in on the reframe piece in this section. When we do this in real life, we would acknowledge (show empathy), clarify to understand, then try a reframe.

Understand: Walk into the Future

Oftentimes, the client will state things the business unit leaders would need from your last reframing question, and we assume that if we address those things, they're going to sign the deal. But the "walk into the future" questions help us understand if anything is missing and not assume an outcome if we go through all the effort—because often, their request can take serious work.

Imagine the client has a concern that we've done our best to understand and to reframe. Walking into the future would entail asking, "Let's say the business unit leaders did buy in. What would you do?" We need to know if the client will say, "I'm going to present it to the business units to get their individual buy off, and if we get that, then we're going to sign the deal," or "That would just help them feel better." In the latter case, we could say, "That's good to hear. What would have to happen for it to move any further than that?" They may clarify: "Once we have the business unit leaders onboard, then we'll have to wrestle through the financials and work through the terms and conditions. At that point, we would consider partnering with you." It helps us find out what else might be out there that would need to be addressed.

Sometimes clients are leading us along without intending to do anything, so "walk into the future" lets us know if that's going on. For example: "For discussion purposes, let's say we resolve your concerns on this issue. What happens? Where would we be?" And if they say, "We also have three other issues with your proposal," we would know either they're not serious or we have a lot of work to do. Either way, it lets us know where we stand.

In the words of an old saying, "If I had an hour to solve a problem, I would spend fifty-five minutes understanding it and five minutes solving it." The principle is that diagnosis precedes prescription. Once we understand what the real concerns are and their criteria for resolution, we can move to resolve.

Resolve

RESOLVE
Mutually resolve the issues at hand.

Once you understand specifically **what they don't like,** and you've explored **what they would like to see** (or hear or experience) that resolves their concern, you can confidently resolve their concern in the way they've asked.

When we thoroughly understand what the client wants to see or hear to resolve their concern, we simply give that information to them. The "give" typically consists of sharing facts and logic, third-party stories, and/or a clear plan. Let's briefly look at each type of information.

Facts and Logic: Sometimes, sharing facts and logic is enough to resolve the concern. Other times, the client just needs to be reminded of the outcomes we agreed to achieve together that can be summed up into three quick From–To statements from our billboard.

Third-Party Stories: Using third-party stories to resolve concerns is probably our favorite approach because stories are so relatable. Recently, we were in the final stages of an opportunity and the client pushed back on a specific aspect of our proposal. We acknowledged, clarified, and then said, "This reminds us of a situation we were involved in recently. Can we share with you what happened with that client and see if it might make sense to do that same thing here?" We then shared a flashback, using Why, What, Why, and it resolved the concern. Third-party stories or flashbacks provide a nice, collaborative way to work through a problem.

A Clear Plan: Once we've gotten this far, clients want us to be prescriptive. We could say, "We recommend taking the following step-by-step approach to resolve this." We can also clearly restate the results they would expect to see. Often a flashforward and a quick summary of why we believe that it makes sense for them to go down this path will resolve the concern: "Here's what the journey looks like, and here's why you're going to get different and better outcomes taking this journey than you might experience somewhere else." Then ask for their thoughts.

An Example of Turning a Yellow Light Green

If you resolve the client's concern, the light will turn green and you can continue moving forward. Let's go through an example that will bring all this together, to resolve a yellow light, using the acknowledge, understand, resolve pattern. Let's imagine we've been having a good discussion about a particular project and then the client says, "We've had bad experiences working with your company in the past. I don't know if I can persuade our team to listen to your new ideas."

Pushback: We've had bad experiences working with your company in the past. I don't know if I can persuade our team to listen to your new ideas.

Acknowledge: I'm sorry to hear you've had bad experiences with us. That's certainly not the reputation we're trying to build. Thanks for your candor. I'd like to repair the reputation we have with you if it's at all possible. (Pause)

Understand: Clarify. Would you be willing to tell me what happened? Do you have the concern or is this a concern others have shared with you? What were the main issues?

Understand: Reframe. Now that I understand what went wrong from your perspective, if we both want this to be diffierent, I realize it's not enough for me to just say it will be different this time. What would you (or others) have to see or hear before you'd have the confidence you'll have a great experience?

Understand: Walk into the Future. I don't know if I can do all those things, but for the moment let's imagine I'm able to address your concerns in the way you've asked. Then where would you be?

Resolve: What I'm hearing is if we can do this and this, then the team will be ready to hear our new ideas, maybe as early as next month. Is that what you're feeling as well? Great, then let's deliver on those two pieces. Here's what I recommend we do.

If the Yellow Light Turns Red

When we've done everything we can to give the client what they've asked for, we still might get to a situation that we just can't resolve. So, what do we do? We stop. Just like in driving, we don't run the red light! We will likely experience much more resistance, and the client's mind may initially be closed to different perspectives and options. So, unless we can create a willingness (in both us and the client) to be open, then our passion to resolve can easily come across as pushy, which will only heighten or create more resistance. So, continue to show empathy and don't rush.

When resolving a red light, try these two additional strategies: "show them the 'ask' is not realistic" and "change their thinking." We'll give you several options for each strategy.

Show Them the "Ask" Is Not Realistic

Use Common Sense

For a variety of reasons, clients sometimes ask for things that are not realistic. In those situations, pause, take a breath, and appeal to the client's sense of reason. Then, offer an alternative.

Example:

Client: You need to cut your fees by 20 percent and keep the scope the same or you're not going to get the contract.

Salesperson: We are excited to work with you on this project. And we want to give you the best value possible. We strongly believe we can get you the results you want, but we simply can't do it at 20 percent less than what we've quoted and keep the scope unchanged. One of these variables would need to change. What we could do is reduce the fees if we pull some things out of scope. The challenge is the full scope is necessary to get you the results you want. What would you like to do?

Client: Well, I don't know what to do. The leadership team isn't going to go for that high of a price, and they want the full results.

Salesperson: What if we were to get creative to solve this challenge together? Let's look at an exchange of value that will make this work for you and keep us whole at the same time. As you know, we just submitted our proposal on the additional project of X in the finance department. If you can help us get that project, then we could reduce our fees on your project by 13 percent and keep scope the same. That way, you will look like a hero with your leadership team, and we will be OK economically between the two projects.

Client: You know, I think I might be able to sell our leadership team on that. Let me see what I can do.

Note: This may not be the way you would choose to resolve this red light. There are many other choices including division of labor (i.e., client does some of the work and we do some of the work), timing of when the work is done, client giving us real references to specific leaders at other companies, payment terms, etc. The key is to engage in authentic, productive conversation with the client to explore possible options to resolve the concern.

Show that No One Could Do It

When clients demand something that is absolutely a deal-breaker, try sharing an example of how no one could satisfy "the ask." Then, if that resonates, work to resolve the concern with high empathy.

Example:

Client: We want you to get started on this project next week. But before you start, we need you to sign our master services agreement, including the indemnification provision.

Salesperson: We're ready to get started and are looking forward to partnering with you. Before we can sign the agreement, we just need to include a reasonable limit on indemnification and liability.

Client: That's ridiculous! Just sign the agreement. It's a huge deal, and you'll be making a lot of money.

Salesperson: Yes, it is a big deal. The challenge is the current indemnification provision gives us unlimited liability. No provider could accept that kind of liability regardless of the size of fees. If something out of our control were to happen, that could literally destroy our company. We are willing to accept overall contractual liability not to exceed three times the fees we get paid on this engagement. That way, we accept an appropriate amount of potential liability for our work, and you are protected in a fair way. If you can make that change, we will sign and get our team ready to start the work next week.

Client: OK. I see what you're saying, and it's reasonable. Let me talk with our legal counsel and see if I can get them to make the change.

To summarize, the first option to address a red light is to show the client their "ask" is unrealistic, which we can do by using common sense or demonstrating that no one could satisfy their "ask." Now, let's dive into a second group of strategies you could use to address red lights, which involve changing the client's thinking.

Change Their Thinking

Share a Different Perspective

Sometimes clients ask for something that would not be in their best interest. In these cases, highlight the negative impact of their request.

Example:

Client: One more thing. We know you do a lot of work in our industry niche, and we need to protect our trade secrets. Before we sign the contract, you'll need to get all of your team members to sign a noncompete agreement stating they won't work with these five competitors for one year after our project is complete.

Salesperson: I definitely hear the concern about the need to protect your trade secrets, and I'm glad you raised it. Your trade secrets are your most important asset in addition to your employees. Here's the challenge. One of the reasons many people choose us is because of our depth and breadth of experience across this industry niche. We bring new ideas, insights, and innovations with us from prior engagements, but we never bring trade secrets. We can't have our team members sign noncompete agreements or we would not be able to continue serving you and your industry. What we can do is sign a strict confidentiality and nondisclosure agreement that covers all team members. That way your trade secrets are protected. Will that work?

Client: We will have to review the language of the agreement with our legal counsel to make sure we are protected.

Salesperson: That makes sense. I'll have our legal counsel send over the standard agreement so your counsel can review the language. Once that agreement gets signed, will you then be ready to sign the contract we've been discussing?

Client: Assuming we reach agreement on the language, then yes, we'll be ready to go.

Offer an Equivalency

Think creatively when a client wants something you can't provide. Look for the need behind the want and offer ways you can achieve the client's desired result in a different way.

Example:

Client: You can only staff this project with people that have a minimum of five years of experience.

Salesperson: Could you help me understand your thinking on the five-year requirement?

Client: I'm not willing to train your people. I'm paying you to bring me top talent. I've found that people with at least five years of experience require very little supervision and do great work. I need this project to succeed no matter what.

Salesperson: Thanks for explaining your thinking. We want this project to succeed as well. I have someone on the team that only has three years of experience. This person outperforms others that have twice the experience. In fact, this individual is the top performer on the team. Would you be willing to include them on the team?

Client: Well, if you personally vouch for this person and agree to replace them with a more experienced person at the first hint of any problems, I guess I'll let the experience requirement slide this time.

Challenge the Relative Importance

When a client demands a particular requirement that you can't satisfy, try challenging the relative importance of the requirement. For example, imagine a client gives you a big list of requirements for a new product you are developing for their company. With creative thinking and flexibility, you're able to reach agreement on all the requirements but one, the delivery date of the product. The client wants it in sixty days. You've considered every possible approach with your team, but due to testing constraints, you've told the client it will take ninety days. Try challenging the relative importance of this specific requirement.

Example:

Client: You have to deliver the product in sixty days or we're not doing business.

Salesperson: What is driving the sixty-day requirement?

Client: This product is the future of our company. The board of directors is demanding that we get this on the market in sixty days. We achieved that development timeframe with one of our other products a couple of years ago. You developers are all the same. You are always putting the brakes on and never move fast enough. We believe if we set the target date at sixty days, it will happen.

Salesperson: Thanks for sharing what's going on with the board. I can see how important this product is for you and the company. We are highly motivated to help develop this new product. It is exciting and is in our sweet spot of experience. We want you to succeed so I'm going to be candid on what we believe is possible, even if it means we don't get the business. We will deliver a high-quality product at a very reasonable cost. The sales forecasts for the new product are significant. We anticipate you will reach twenty million dollars in sales with a high gross margin within the first three months of market launch. You will dominate your market segment and will continue to grow at a more than 25 percent compound annual growth rate for the next five years. This product is more complex than the previous product you developed. We have run every scenario possible. If we accelerate the timeline to sixty days, we won't have sufficient time to pressure test the product and it will fail, jeopardizing all the outcomes I just mentioned. Is the sixty-day requirement more important than ensuring you're successful in the short and long term? At ninety days, we feel highly confident the product will be ready and successful.

Client: That's really hard to hear. Let me go back to the board and see if I can get them to change their minds.

EXIT THE OPPORTUNITY GRACEFULLY

In the above examples, we were able to resolve the client's red lights, turn them to green, and move forward toward closure. In real life, that doesn't always happen. There are times when we don't reach an agreement that works for us and the client; in those cases, we need to be willing to exit the opportunity. There are two aspects to exiting an opportunity gracefully.

First, we need to be sincerely willing to walk away from the opportunity. Not in a flippant way. Not as a tactic. Rather, we simply determine that under the currently discussed terms and conditions, it just won't work for us. So, we let the client know we need to withdraw from the opportunity, and we wish them the very best. Often, that's when the client will change their mind and decide to work together with us to resolve their red light in a mutually beneficial way. Other times, it won't change a thing.

Second, when it becomes clear that we really are going to walk away, we need to do it with grace and class. Question: Is it possible to exit an opportunity and still build a relationship? Absolutely, if we keep our composure and let the client know we genuinely wish them success in their endeavors. We can also leave the door open to future communication if something changes and they need our help. A client of ours, Alejandra, experienced a $67 million win by exiting an opportunity gracefully and leaving the door open. She was proposing on a technology transformation project with a financial services company headquartered in Mexico City. Everything was going great until she reviewed her pricing schedule with the company. The company insisted she cut the price by 40 percent to match the quote from a local vendor or her firm was not going to get the business. Alejandra did everything she could to resolve the red light, but the client wouldn't budge off their demand. So, Alejandra gracefully exited the opportunity. As she was exiting, she told the CEO of the financial services company, "I sincerely hope you succeed with your project. I know it is vital to the success of your company. Will you please make sure the local vendor does these five things?" She then gave him the list. "If at any point you get concerned or things aren't going according to plan, please call me and I'll give you free advice." Six months later, she got a call from the CEO. He said, "Alejandra, we are in big trouble. The project is not going well, and I'm very worried. Can you please come meet me in my office tomorrow?" Alejandra met with the CEO and ultimately got the contract at the price she had originally quoted—approximately $67 million.

Now that we've walked through the Acknowledge, Understand, Resolve framework, note that not all the elements of the framework are necessary, or even appropriate, in every situation to resolve a client's yellow or red light. Think of the Acknowledge, Understand, Resolve framework as a menu of different skills and choices that we can use when appropriate. Take these elements, practice them, and try different versions until you feel comfortable that you have a variety of options to address most concerns or questions.

Navigating the traffic lights of an opportunity is the essence and very heart of validating and co-creating. As we drive through the intersections of an opportunity and encounter yellow or red lights, it gives us the chance to change and deepen our relationship with the client. Clients not only appreciate our willingness to solve an issue, but more importantly, our ability to do it together. Some of the best relationships we've built with clients have come not when everything was going perfectly in a sales pursuit, but when tough issues came up.

The principle behind navigating traffic lights is to welcome them. Look at every traffic light as a buying signal. You just need to navigate each one the right way. Slow down and stop when necessary and connect with the client. It's all about having a conversation, leaving arrogance aside, and bringing a humble, confident mindset that we likely can work this out if we have the client's best interests at heart. And when we can't, we exit gracefully and leave the door open.

As we conclude Part 2, we've now shared the six Strikingly Different skills the world's top sales performers use to connect and engage with their clients (Part 1) and validate and co-create the client's message house and related solutions (Part 2). You might use any number of these skills in a single sales conversation as well as throughout the entire sales cycle. In the next chapter, we'll show you how a salesperson might artfully weave these skills throughout a middle-stage conversation to achieve Strikingly Different results.

Exercise:

Think of specific client scenarios. Write down two yellow lights and one red light and how you will acknowledge, understand, and resolve each one.

Client Statement:

____

____

____

____

Your Response:

____

____

____

____

Acknowledge:

Understand:

Clarify:

Reframe:

Walk Into the Future:

Resolve:

KEY INSIGHTS FOR SKILL 6

- Change your thinking about sales traffic lights. Look at them as signals that the client is interested in buying what you have to sell. The different lights just need to be understood and navigated the right way.
- Navigating yellow and red lights requires us to slow down or stop, show empathy, and engage in real human-to-human dialogue.
- Navigating all three colors of traffic lights will help you find and close the gaps in the message house until it looks like, feels like, and becomes the client's message house. That's when the client and you win together.
- To become proficient at this skill:
    - Listen for various green, yellow, and red lights in your daily life.
    - Practice in everyday conversations with your coworkers, clients, neighbors, and family.

PULLING IT ALL TOGETHER

Throughout this book, we've discussed how to connect and engage with clients through the message house and its elements—billboards, movie trailers, flashbacks and flashforwards, and Why Us! differentiators—then validate and co-create the message house continuously throughout the sales process. Granted, this may seem like a lot to juggle, but the more you use these elements and their associated tools, the more you'll seamlessly and flexibly incorporate them into your sales interactions.

Let's see how a salesperson might pull everything together in a middle-stage sales conversation. The dialogue below is based on a real-life scenario of one of our clients with selected details changed to protect confidentiality.

Context for Middle-Stage Sales Meeting with CIO of Government Agency

SALESPERSON:
JESSICA

CLIENT:
VIJAY

Scenario: Jessica, a sales executive with a cloud-based software company, is about to start a live-online meeting with Vijay, the chief information officer (CIO) of a government agency. Both she and the client will be on camera.

Jessica has already had several meetings with individuals who report to Vijay to build the business case for implementing a comprehensive, cloud-based software solution at the agency. She built their message house (see following page) and has been validating and co-creating it based on her meetings and research. She seems to have good support among Vijay's team. Now, Jessica needs to get buy-in from the CIO. Jessica's goal is to get Vijay's perspective on the issues his team is facing and, assuming her solution can resolve those issues, schedule a full software demo with Vijay and his team.

Jessica set up the meeting with Vijay on a phone call where she used a compelling movie trailer that piqued Vijay's interest. Vijay talked with his team to get their perspective and is looking forward to the meeting. At the same time, he has at least one concern.

Jessica moves the meeting forward as illustrated on the following pages.

Strikingly Different Message House for Government Agency

CAPTURE ATTENTION

MAIN HEADLINE

Transform from a frustrated and disconnected employee base working remotely to an engaged and productive workforce with the tools they need to work from anywhere.

CREATE EXCITEMENT

FROM-TO SUB HEADLINE 1	FROM-TO SUB HEADLINE 2	FROM-TO SUB HEADLINE 3
Move from disparate systems that create a lack of visibility across teams to a fully integrated system that provides a 360-degree view of every citizen/case.	Evolve employees from feeling frustrated with unreliable systems and applications to being fully enabled with mobile and digital applications.	Resolve cases in hours rather than days, leading to big increases in citizen and employee satisfaction.

BUILD CONFIDENCE

PAST SUCCESS STORY (FLASHBACK 1)

Agency 1

Why did client need help: Disconnected systems, high citizen and employee complaints.

What we did/achieved: Implemented flexible remote workforce platform. Agency saw 69% drop in citizen complaints and resolved cases in three hours versus nine days pre-implementation.

PAST SUCCESS STORY (FLASHBACK 2)

Agency 2

Why did client need help: High employee complaints and turnover, high citizen complaints, remote workforce issues.

What we did/achieved: Changed process and implemented new flexible platform. Reduced employee turnover by 39%, reduced citizen complaints by 77%, resolved cases in five hours versus eleven days before implementation.

FUTURE SUCCESS STORY (FLASHFORWARD)

Why change:
Frustrated and disconnected employee base with high turnover and high citizen complaints.

What's the journey:
Six-month implementation in three phases.

Why do it:
To realize the future state vision in From-To sub headlines above.

BECOME ESSENTIAL

WHY US! DIFFERENTIATOR 1	WHY US! DIFFERENTIATOR 2	WHY US! DIFFERENTIATOR 3
One Stop Shop Solve people, process, and tech issues vs. just tech.	Flexible Platform Flexible choices vs. rigid "one way fits all."	Dedicated Agency Team Each team member is 100% focused on agencies vs. part-time consultants from other industries.
WHAT WE WILL DO WITH DIFFERENTIATOR 1 Run comprehensive diagnostic on Day One to determine your unique people, process, and tech priorities.	**WHAT WE WILL DO WITH DIFFERENTIATOR 2** Configure mobile and digital platform the way your team wants to use it.	**WHAT WE WILL DO WITH DIFFERENTIATOR 3** Dedicated agency team will focus on citizen needs and issues.
WHY DIFFERENTIATOR 1 MATTERS Decrease risk and increase speed to outcomes.	**WHY DIFFERENTIATOR 2 MATTERS** Increase employee engagement, decrease their frustration and related turnover.	**WHY DIFFERENTIATOR 3 MATTERS** Increase citizen satisfaction and net promoter scores.

R+D+M=STRIKINGLY DIFFERENT

Sample Middle-Stage Conversation
USING ALL SIX SKILLS

SALESPERSON: JESSICA

WHY **STRIKINGLY DIFFERENT?**

CLIENT: VIJAY

Jessica: Vijay, I've been looking forward to this meeting since we chatted last week.

Vijay: I've been looking forward to it as well. I've had a chance to debrief with my team members. So far, they seem to be supportive of the ideas you've shared with them.

Jessica: I'm glad you've debriefed with your team members. They've been very helpful in getting me up to speed on what's going on at the agency.

> **Jessica connects in a friendly way and acknowledges Vijay's team has been helpful.**

I would like to take just two minutes to share what we discussed last week at a high level, get your thoughts on that since you've had a week to think about it, and then ***have you share some of the specific challenges you've been experiencing with your people working remotely. Would that be okay?***

> **Jessica sets the stage that she is going to share the main points of her movie trailer (advocacy), sets up the discovery portion of the meeting (inquiry), and gets Vijay's buy-in to proceed.**

Vijay: Sure, that sounds good.

Jessica: As I mentioned last week, we're seeing several top government agencies do three things to ***transform from a frustrated and disconnected employee base working remotely, to an engaged and productive workforce with the tools they need to work from anywhere.***

> **Jessica quickly connects back to the movie trailer she used last week to get the meeting with Vijay by sharing the main From–To HEADLINE.**

Sample Middle-Stage Conversation
USING ALL SIX SKILLS

SALESPERSON:
JESSICA

WHY
STRIKINGLY DIFFERENT?

CLIENT:
VIJAY

Salesperson (Jessica): First, they are moving ***from disparate systems that create a lack of visibility across teams to a fully integrated system that provides a 360-degree view of every citizen/case.***

Second, employees in these agencies have evolved ***from feeling frustrated with unreliable systems and applications to being fully enabled*** with mobile and digital applications.

And third, these agencies are ***resolving their cases in hours rather than days,*** leading to big increases in both citizen and employee satisfaction.

Vijay, what are your thoughts?

Why strikingly different? **Jessica shares three From-To SUB HEADLINES from her movie trailer and creates clear contrast between Vijay's status quo and a different and better future state.**

Her headlines are relevant, distinct, and memorable.

After sharing her movie trailer in less than two minutes, Jessica gets the client's reaction before moving forward.

Client (Vijay): All three of those actions/outcomes resonate with me. My team is feeling a lot of frustration with the current environment. It's clearly affecting their productivity and quality of work.

Sample Middle-Stage Conversation
USING ALL SIX SKILLS

SALESPERSON: JESSICA

WHY STRIKINGLY DIFFERENT?

CLIENT: VIJAY

Jessica: ***I'm sorry your team is having a hard time.*** And you're not alone. Every agency is dealing with similar issues right now. ***Having seen great results at several other agencies, I'm excited to share the possibilities for your agency.***

Vijay: I would like to hear the possibilities.

Jessica: Before we jump into those ideas and examples, ***can we spend a few minutes exploring the specific challenges you are facing, and the goals you need to achieve?*** Then I would love to share our experiences in detail, to see if we can help.

Why strikingly different? **Jessica shows empathy, plants a seed about great results that are possible, then transitions into the most important part of the meeting—learning about Vijay's challenges and goals. Note: This is a key inflection point where Jessica moves from advocacy to inquiry to find the gaps in the message house.**

Vijay: Sure. Let me add to what my team has already shared with you. From my perspective, here are the specific challenges we're dealing with right now in this remote work environment...

And these are our most important goals ...

Jessica: It's interesting to hear just ***how similar your experience has been to several other agencies*** we have worked with recently.

Would it make sense for me to share one or two of those experiences to give you some insights as you consider a similar journey?

Why strikingly different? **Jessica spends 10–15 minutes asking questions while Vijay provides answers and details about his agency's challenges and goals. Then, recognizing another key inflection point and the need to do a bit more advocacy, Jessica asks if Vijay would like to hear a flashback story.**

Vijay: Yes, please do.

Sample Middle-Stage Conversation
USING ALL SIX SKILLS

SALESPERSON:
JESSICA

WHY
STRIKINGLY DIFFERENT?

CLIENT:
VIJAY

Salesperson (Jessica): I'm thinking about one particular agency. I'll just share ***why they needed to change*** (their challenges and goals), ***what they did, learned, and achieved,*** and ***why that might matter to you in your situation...***

Why Strikingly Different? Jessica shares a Why, What, Why flashback story that is relevant to Vijay's top challenges and goals.

Salesperson (Jessica): ***Vijay, what's your reaction to what I just shared?***

Why Strikingly Different? Jessica pauses and gets Vijay's reaction and thoughts before proceeding.

Client (Vijay): That's a good example. It felt like you were describing quite a bit of our situation.

Salesperson (Jessica): It's good to hear that although there are differences, you feel there is clear relevancy to your organization and what you are trying to do. Because I believe that we can help your agency ***transform from a frustrated and disconnected employee base working remotely, to an engaged and productive work-force with the tools they need to work from anywhere.***

Do you believe it's possible to capture the three outcomes we mentioned earlier, those being ***1, 2, 3***?

Why Strikingly Different? Jessica connects back to the main HEADLINE and then asks Vijay if he believes it's possible to achieve the three outcomes (SUB HEADLINES) mentioned earlier in the meeting.

Client (Vijay): It sounds like it. Look, I've got to be honest with you. I really like your fresh, new ideas for our agency. However, from what I hear, you are really expensive. I'm not sure I can get the rest of the executive team to buy in. Why are you so expensive?

Sample Middle-Stage Conversation
USING ALL SIX SKILLS

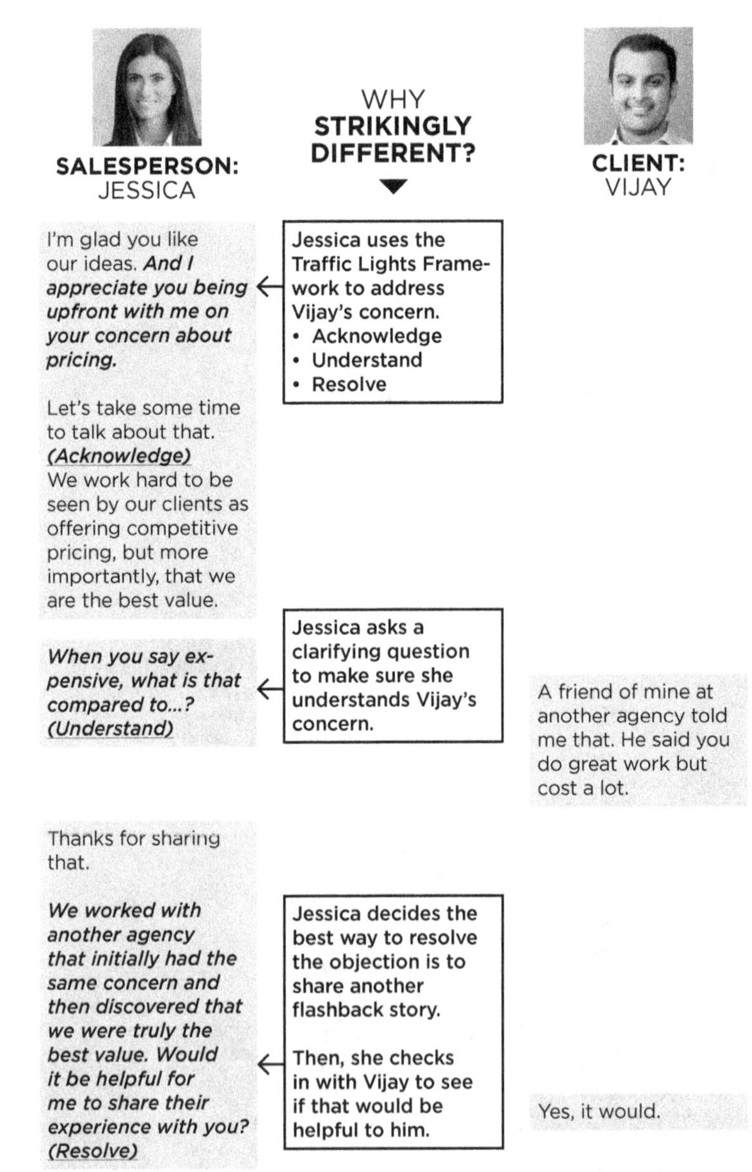

Sample Middle-Stage Conversation
USING ALL SIX SKILLS

SALESPERSON: JESSICA

WHY **STRIKINGLY DIFFERENT?**

CLIENT: VIJAY

SALESPERSON: JESSICA	WHY STRIKINGLY DIFFERENT?	CLIENT: VIJAY
This other agency also loved our ideas and innovative solutions to their challenges. ***They wanted the outcomes we could deliver but were worried about the pricing.*** ***(Why)***	← **Jessica shares a flashback of another agency that had a similar pricing concern to resolve Vijay's concern. Her goal was to help Vijay see that her company is the best value for the desired outcomes.**	
So, ***we worked together with them to do a detailed analysis of alternatives, comparing costs, risks, return on investment (ROI) and outcomes.*** It became clear to that agency that we were the safest and best choice. ***They engaged us, and we delivered the promised outcomes on time and on budget.*** They told us at the end of the implementation that ***they would do it again because of the significant value they received. (What)***		
We can deliver the same value to your agency. (Why)		
We would be happy to connect you with their CIO so you can talk with her if you would like.	← **Jessica offers to connect Vijay with the CIO of the other agency. This boosts Jessica's credibility and increases Vijay's confidence that he should continue to move the process forward.**	Yes, that would be really helpful.

Sample Middle-Stage Conversation
USING ALL SIX SKILLS

SALESPERSON:
JESSICA

WHY
STRIKINGLY DIFFERENT?

CLIENT:
VIJAY

Vijay: So, I have another question for you. What makes your company different from the other remote workforce software vendors out there?

Jessica uses the Why Us! differentiation framework to answer Vijay's question. She contrasts each difference against something else *(Why)*. She describes what her team will do with each difference *(What)* and why that matters to Vijay and the agency *(Why)*.

Jessica: Great question. As it relates to solving your challenges, three things come to mind: 1. ***one-stop shop,*** 2. ***flexible platform,*** and 3. ***dedicated agency team.***

1. We solve people, process, ***and*** tech issues. We'll run a diagnostic to determine priorities on Day 1, ***decreasing risk and increasing speed to outcomes.***

2. We give flexible choices ***vs.*** one way fits all. We'll configure the mobile and digital platform the way your team wants to use it. This will ***increase employee engagement, decrease their frustration, and reduce turnover.***

3. Each team member is 100% dedicated to agency work ***vs.*** being spread across industries. The team will focus on citizen issues, helping you increase satisfaction and NPS scores.

Based on this, do you believe we're different?

Jessica asks Vijay whether he believes her company is different. This opens the dialogue up. In this case, Vijay believes her company is different. However, if her stated differences had somehow missed the mark, this question would help her discover what she needs to adjust to be different and better for Vijay's agency.

Vijay: What you just shared makes a lot of sense. Yes, it sure seems like your company is different in a good way.

Sample Middle-Stage Conversation
USING ALL SIX SKILLS

SALESPERSON:
JESSICA

WHY
STRIKINGLY DIFFERENT?

CLIENT:
VIJAY

Vijay: What do you recommend our next steps should be to get others of my executive team on board and to help me challenge their thinking?

Jessica: Here's what I recommend.

First, ***I'll connect you with the CIO of the other agency.*** Second, let's schedule a demonstration of our remote workforce solution with you and the executive team. ***We'll make sure to highlight the outcomes your agency can achieve and leave ample time for "what if" scenario discussion.*** Third, I suggest we work closely with you and your staff over the next two weeks to ***co-develop the business case with your actual metrics and measures.*** Then, you can present it to the executive team. At that point you and the team can decide if you want to move forward or not.

Why strikingly different? Jessica shares a quick flashforward focusing primarily on what the immediate journey looks like (next steps) to address Vijay's question.

How does that sound?

Why strikingly different? Jessica transfers motivation to Vijay.

Vijay: That sounds like a great plan. Thank you for being so prepared today.

Jessica: You're welcome! I'm excited to work with you and am confident your agency will achieve the outcomes we've discussed.

Conclusion: WINNING THE SALE

As we featured at the beginning of this book, our client Mark embraced the formula and skills of Strikingly Different Selling to win one of the largest deals of his career. Over the course of two months, Mark overhauled his approach to the client, his message, and his delivery to be far more effective, concise, and clear. And it worked.

The key, according to Mark, was looking at everything he and his team were going to do and say through the RDM lens again and again every step of the way. Was this element relevant? Was it distinct? Was it memorable? Were they using the client's words, phrases, and language? Were they framing the issues in the way the client would say them?

Mark particularly pushed himself on the From–To statements—juxtaposing the current state versus future state—until he found the unique differentiators. As he and his team prepared for the two and a half hour orals presentation against three other firms, they constantly asked themselves, *How can we stand out so when our client is having a coffee break or at dinner, they're talking about our story, not the competitors'? How can we be even more RDM?* They repeated "RDM" almost like a song.

In the end, Mark's (tall!) message house looked like this:

CAPTURE ATTENTION

MAIN HEADLINE

Empower IT as an indispensable, leading-edge strategic partner to the business.

CREATE EXCITEMENT

FROM-TO SUB HEADLINE 1	FROM-TO SUB HEADLINE 2	FROM-TO SUB HEADLINE 3
Improve business process compliance massively from present levels to >98% from Day Zero, thereby maximizing the business case benefits.	Accelerate IT from the current state to a new technology-enabled proactive growth engine within the first twelve months.	Move from a manual, high incident-volume support service to a proactive, hyper-automated service where "the best ticket in the world is the one that does not exist."

BUILD CONFIDENCE

PAST SUCCESS STORY (FLASHBACK 1)

Global media company

Why did client need help: Cumbersome processes, costs too high, productivity too low.

What we did/achieved: Implemented intelligent ERP system in Operations, Accounting, Procurement, Maintenance, and Sales functions. Client achieved $129 million in cost savings, reduced number of unique reports from 4,000 to 70, improved productivity by 45%.

PAST SUCCESS STORY (FLASHBACK 2)

Asia-Pacific-based telecommunications company

Why did client need help: Outdated technology, highly manual processes, high costs.

What we did/achieved: Operated end-to-end AMS for the past five years. Improved process compliance from 83% to 99%, reduced maintenance tickets from thousands to dozens, and transformed IT from routine tasks to growth strategies.

FUTURE SUCCESS STORY (FLASHFORWARD)

Why change:
Simplify and standardize processes so client can focus on strategic growth objectives.

What's the journey:
Three-year outsourcing partnership. The journey includes enabling digital transformation with a four-prong approach: 1) Limit risk; 2) Move key functions offshore; 3) Automate key business processes; 4) Innovate continuously.

Why do it:
To realize the future state vision in From-To sub headlines above.

BECOME ESSENTIAL

WHY US! DIFFERENTIATOR 1	WHY US! DIFFERENTIATOR 2	WHY US! DIFFERENTIATOR 3
Hyper Automation Platform Integrated, self-healing automation stack vs. disparate AI apps.	**Continuous Innovation & Co-creation** Joint collaboration at our Innovation centers and full access to our internal IT learning boards vs. limited access.	**Team with Deep Industry Experience** Each team member brings several years of relevant AMS experience in your industry vs. pulling people from other industries.
WHAT WE WILL DO WITH DIFFERENTIATOR 1 Implement platform on Day Zero, unleashing desired outcomes.	**WHAT WE WILL DO WITH DIFFERENTIATOR 2** Conduct joint innovation sessions with the first month and provide access to learning boards starting on Day Zero.	**WHAT WE WILL DO WITH DIFFERENTIATOR 3** Implement risk-based transition plan, strict governance and monitor business-critical KPIs.
WHY DIFFERENTIATOR 1 MATTERS Decrease costs and increase productivity at the same time.	**WHY DIFFERENTIATOR 2 MATTERS** Capture new sources of growth in parallel with transforming core operations through digitization.	**WHY DIFFERENTIATOR 3 MATTERS** Mitigate transition and business operations risks with ability to solve problems immediately.

R+D+M=STRIKINGLY DIFFERENT

As Mark and his team put the final proposal together, they realized that even the *way* they presented could be RDM. In Mark's firm, his sophisticated colleagues relied on detailed PowerPoint decks with hundreds of slides; they couldn't imagine being without them. But Mark and his team went into the presentation without a single slide. They presented their core Strikingly Different messages using microsites (web pages). They spent most of their time in a novel use of the flashforward, using the microsites to show several "days in the life," a very experiential approach that helped the client see what it would feel like to interact with their solution.

At the end of the presentation, the client executives told Mark and his team that their proposal surprised them—it was fresh and crisp and bold and focused on what was most important to them.

Now Mark is an enthusiastic champion. He's shared the formula and skills of Strikingly Different selling with multiple sales teams and individuals around the globe and has seen numerous wins come as a result.

As with Mark, our goal is to help you become Strikingly Different through a message house that captures your vision of how you can help your clients achieve different and better results. Throughout this process, you still may have to comply with a request for proposal (RFP), but you never want to lose sight of the message house. It's a tested, flexible structure that can endure the constant changes in the selling environment, including the recent transition to online selling (remember, if you are struggling with this transition, as many understandably are, we've included an appendix of best practices for online sales interactions).

Strikingly Different Message House

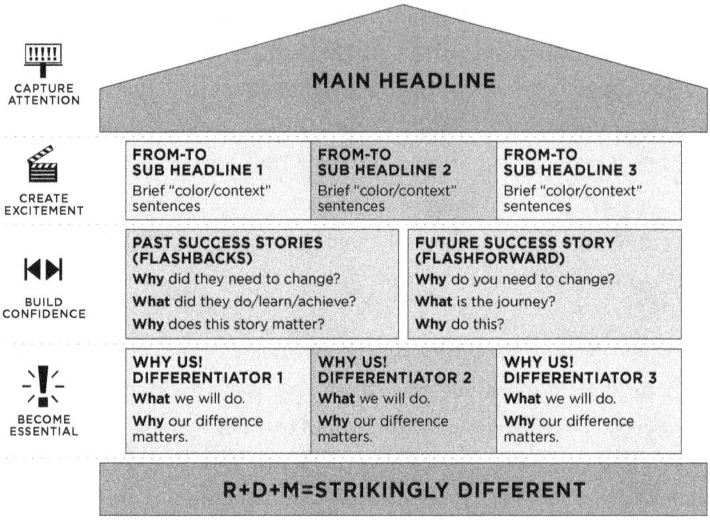

CAPTURE ATTENTION

MAIN HEADLINE

CREATE EXCITEMENT

FROM-TO SUB HEADLINE 1	FROM-TO SUB HEADLINE 2	FROM-TO SUB HEADLINE 3
Brief "color/context" sentences	Brief "color/context" sentences	Brief "color/context" sentences

BUILD CONFIDENCE

PAST SUCCESS STORIES (FLASHBACKS)	FUTURE SUCCESS STORY (FLASHFORWARD)
Why did they need to change?	**Why** do you need to change?
What did they do/learn/achieve?	**What** is the journey?
Why does this story matter?	**Why** do this?

BECOME ESSENTIAL

WHY US! DIFFERENTIATOR 1	WHY US! DIFFERENTIATOR 2	WHY US! DIFFERENTIATOR 3
What we will do.	**What** we will do.	**What** we will do.
Why our difference matters.	**Why** our difference matters.	**Why** our difference matters.

R+D+M=STRIKINGLY DIFFERENT

When we build a message house, it's essentially a blueprint. Our vision starts as a rough sketch, with maybe just a roof and the foundation of being relevant, distinct, and memorable. As you share this sketch, you and the client push up walls, raise the roof, change the shape of the house, and add architectural elements. When you arrive at the end, you have a blueprint for the ideal house, hopefully one that the client wants to live in. Your ability to tell the final story as "our" story (yours and the client's) is the key.

But here's an important point: the house is not yet constructed. When we say that our house has become the client's house, it means the design for that house is exactly what the client wants, as if we're on the same team. At the end of the sales process, we want the client to invite us to *build or deliver* the house we've helped them architect to achieve those different and better outcomes. The house could be a product or a service, or whatever constitutes the type of solution you sell to your clients.

THE FOUNDATION: RELEVANT + DISTINCT + MEMORABLE

We want to leave you with a final thought around RDM, the basis of our message house, this book, and the Strikingly Different skills. As we've discussed, we use this lens to evaluate every message we present to the client. Are we focused on what matters most to the client? Do the words, phrases, and approach tie back to their issues, challenges, and goals? Are we showing something different and better to the client than the status quo? Is the message easy to share, hard to forget? Because the stories we tell become currency inside the client's organization, and how that currency is invested or squandered will determine whether we win or lose.

But we can—and should—go beyond applying RDM to our message houses. We can also apply the formula to ourselves as sellers. Ask yourself: Am *I* Strikingly Different? Am I relevant? Am I distinct? Am I different and better in the way that I show up? Is the way I engage online different and better? Am I easy to engage with? Am I memorable? We guarantee that Mark's client was talking about their memorable experience with his team as contrasted with the three other firms who likely relied on traditional slide decks and seller-focused presentations.

If you allow it, RDM and the six skills will change you. They will change how you think, what you say, and what you do, resulting in shorter sales cycles, better opportunities, stronger client relationships, and bigger results. You don't need to be perfect to get remarkable results. You just need to be directionally correct. Small changes make a big difference. Good luck on your journey.

Appendix: CONDUCTING EXCELLENT ONLINE CLIENT MEETINGS

In the middle of a recent online conversation, the client executive's cat jumped up on the desk, just to the side of what we could see on camera. The cat, with raised tail, sauntered over to the executive and turned to face her. What were we looking at for the next few minutes? That's right, the cat's backside. The experience was definitely memorable, but not in the way we're talking about in this book, and not in the way you want online.

Technology should be transparent, so you don't think about the fact that you're using it. This is especially true of online meetings—the technology should be transparent so the person you're talking to doesn't notice it; they just see you and the information you're sharing.

In this appendix, we explore why online meetings fail, as well as a formula for making your online meetings so Strikingly Different that your clients will compare every other meeting to your meetings and wonder why they aren't as good.

WHY DO ONLINE MEETINGS FAIL?

The primary reason online meetings fail is because of the prevailing mindset that online meetings are inferior to in-person meetings. We've all attended an online meeting where the internet connection is unstable, or the person can't get online, or you need to download an update before the meeting can start, or the client can't get off mute, or you're distracted when the dog starts barking at the delivery person, or a child runs through the background, or one of our personal favorites, heads disappear in the virtual background.

Let's offer you a different perspective. Have you ever had an in-person meeting at a restaurant? Or in a conference room? Or at a coffee shop? Or at a business event? If you have, you likely have experienced the same failure points that you experienced online, just manifested a little differently. The projector you were going to show your presentation on doesn't work, or the cable connection is "unstable" and your presentation keeps flickering off and on, or the client doesn't show for an important meeting, or you're in a restaurant and a large tray of dishes crashes to the floor just as your customer is about to agree to the deal, or you're at a social event and someone spills their drink on you, or you are in the middle of delivering a presentation and your computer starts smoking and then bursts into flames (that really happened).

Did you swear off in-person meetings at that point? Did you decide that it just wasn't worth the time or effort? No. Why? Because of your mindset. You knew you would have distractions, interruptions, and potential technical failures, and therefore you weren't thrown off. In fact, you most likely planned for the potential disasters and were able to pull off the meeting despite these distractions. You were a hero. You weren't stopped by what was because you knew what could be.

The main reason online meetings fail is the same reason in-person meetings fail—lack of planning, preconditioning, and practice. When you plan for the distractions, interruptions, and potential technical failures, you avoid most of them.

FOLLOW THE FORMULA FOR SUCCESS

Keep two things in mind when conducting live-online meetings. First, meetings are excellent only when the client thinks they are excellent. And the reason you're having a meeting in the first place is because the client has a decision to make, and to make the decision, they need information. Simply put, the purpose of any client meeting is to enable your client to make a decision. Period. If there isn't a decision to make, then you don't need to meet.

Second, meetings online are not virtual meetings. Oxford Language's definition of virtual is "not physically existing as such but made by software to appear to do so."[4] You and the client physically exist. You are not fake, and your client is not fake. Neither you nor your client are represented by avatars. You are in a real-life meeting that happens to be online. We call them *live-online* meetings. The reason we emphasize this point is because when you call it a "virtual meeting," you subscribe to the mindset that online meetings are inferior and therefore cannot accomplish anything close to what in-person meetings can accomplish. The only thing that makes an online meeting different from an in-person meeting is the medium of communication. In person, you use vocal cords, airwaves, and eyeballs. Online, you use microphones, speakers, and cameras. Online meetings are not imitating real meetings; they are real meetings.

Now that we have the right foundational mindset, let's get into the formula for online meeting success. To succeed at online meetings, follow this formula:

4 "Virtual." Oxford University Press. 2021. https://www.google.com/search?q=virtual+definition&rlz=1C1CHBF_enUS872US872&oq=virtual+definition&aqs=chrome..69i57j0l9.2159j1j7&sourceid=chrome&ie=UTF-8

P^3 - I = SUCCESS

(Plan + Precondition + Practice) - Interference = Success

There are **four "E's"** to planning online meeting success:

1. **Engagement**
2. **Environment**
3. **Equipment**
4. **End in Mind**

PLAN: ENGAGEMENT

When you engage with people online, you have tools available that you don't have during in-person meetings, giving you a great deal of power to enable your client to make a decision:

- **Screen Share**
- **Chat**
- **Annotate**
- **Breakout**
- **Polls**

Whatever online platform you use, you will have tools to engage your client in a meaningful discussion about their needs. The question is how you will use the tools to engage the client. For example, if you are meeting with one person, you may only need to share your screen or have them share theirs. If you have multiple participants, you may use screen share, chat, breakouts, and polls. If you are brainstorming with a client, you may annotate a white board to emphasize text, or draw or circle pictures. The key to every one of these tools is that you *plan* how and when to use it to enable the client to make a decision.

Warning: If you don't need the tool, don't use it. The meeting is not a place for you to show off your online prowess. You may be excited to use a certain tool to wow the client, but if it doesn't help the client make a decision, the tool becomes interference. Remember that these tools are assisting you and are not the main show. Don't stay in screen share the entire meeting. After you have shared the document or slide and it is no longer needed, stop sharing your screen. Continuing to share a slide when it is no longer needed is interference.

Recently we were preparing for a critical "go forward" online meeting in which the client was deciding whether to implement our multi-million dollar solution. The client's decision-making committee was eighteen people strong. Before we met with them, we had a planning meeting to determine what online tools we would use to enable the client to make the best possible implementation decision.

We determined that we would start by using screen share to communicate a couple of key points. Then we would utilize chat to solicit responses and questions from the committee. From the responses in the chat, we would call on people to expand on a point or clarify a question.

By the way, to get verbal responses from people in online meetings, you call people by name to respond. The reason? Have you been in an online meeting and had a question asked to everyone? What happened after the question was asked? Everyone probably sat silently for several awkward seconds, then two or three people responded at once, which then led to a tennis match of, "You can go first, Mariana." "No, you go first." "No, I was ready to hear what you had to say." "No really, I insist you go first." Then both people start talking at the same time again. You avoid this awkwardness by calling on people or have them raise their hand—literally or using a platform feature.

After the initial opening discussion, we planned to use breakout rooms so smaller groups of people could discuss how they would modify or make the implementation better. After hearing from each of the groups, we planned to use a poll to get everyone's opinion on whether the implementation was complete and clear. We also planned to share a document where we captured, in real time, the notes from each group. We planned every minute of the meeting, using online tools and features not available in person, and the planning paid off. The client signed the contract.

We debriefed after the meeting and realized that we could not have done in person what we did online. The online tools made the client's decision-making process efficient and effective. It also gave everyone an equal voice.

Have you been in an in-person client meeting where the decision being made is largely influenced by what one person says? In that setting, when a critical question is asked, all heads turn toward the person in the room who wields the greatest political power and whatever that person says is how the other people vote. In an online meeting, that political power is greatly diminished by using anonymous polls or the chat feature, which gives everyone the opportunity to weigh in, producing a much better decision.

PLAN: ENVIRONMENT

Your online environment is made up of everything people see when you are on camera and everything they hear through your microphone. You want to plan your environment so that the client can make a distraction-free decision. That doesn't mean you need to make it void of decoration, nor do you need to worry if all you have is a plain wall. You can use virtual backgrounds (and in this case "virtual" is the correct word to use because the background is fake) but use caution. If you use a virtual background, invest in an inexpensive greenscreen and lighting, which you can find online. They will give you the best results to avoid disappearing arms, fingers, and ears as you move around. If you can't obtain additional equipment, situate yourself in front of a plain, one-color wall, with light illuminating your face and the wall.

As you plan your environment, remember the last meeting you had in a restaurant. The restaurant was most likely filled with people talking, laughing, and moving. Also, servers were waiting tables, clearing dishes, and processing payments. Somehow amidst all this distraction you were able to focus on your client, hearing their words, asking them questions, and eventually arriving at a decision. How? You expected interruptions.

When planning your online meeting, do what you can to minimize interruptions, distractions, and diversions; however, they will happen. You are probably working at a home you share with other people. Tell them about your plan for the day and the client meetings you have. Try putting a sign on the door, like the light on the outside of a recording studio, indicating that you are "in session." If applicable, put the dog in another part of the house or outside, and hang a sign over the doorbell asking people to knock. But even with these measures in place, there will still be unplanned interruptions. And that's OK.

Some of the most memorable live-online moments for us have come when we met someone's child, partner, or favorite pet that wandered into the room in the middle of a meeting. One moment that stands out happened during a live, national webcast when the presenter's wife walked into the room. The presenter was in the middle of delivering an important point to the 450 people in the meeting. (Doesn't it seem that is when most unplanned environmental interruptions happen...right when you're making a big point?) After retrieving something from the office, she came over and gave the presenter a kiss on the cheek. The presenter introduced his wife to everyone in the meeting, she waved, said hi, then left the room.

That moment has been permanently etched in our minds because the presenter didn't get ruffled, angry, or frustrated. He graciously accepted his partner's affection, introduced her, and we, every one of us, witnessed a moment that we never would have seen in an office, conference room, or convention hall. When you enter an online meeting, you don't leave your world behind—you invite others into it. You are also invited into the other person's world, which gives you a unique opportunity to have an even more intimate relationship.

We have heard sales professionals say that in-person meetings build relationships, but online meetings do not. We disagree. Your online meeting can be much more personal and relationship-building than an in-person meeting in an office could ever be. Clients get to see your interests, meet your children or friends, and sometimes even witness small acts of affection from those you care about most.

Framing

Imagine sitting in a movie theater with your popcorn and soda when the movie starts, and all you can see on the big screen is the top of the actor's head or their face from the nose up. When the scene switches, you see up their nose. In the next scene, the actors are only on the left side of the screen or looking down on you from the top of the screen. How would you feel? Would it be uncomfortable? Would you spend most of your time wanting to move the camera to get the people on screen? Would this be distracting and cause interference? Yes!

Your organization has spent a lot of money over time to make, produce, and distribute the products and services you represent. Now when you are ready to show and discuss those products or services, how you frame yourself on camera is critical to giving the audience, your clients, the most enjoyable experience and the best opportunity to make a distraction-free decision.

When you meet people in person, you naturally frame them like the following picture in your mind.

When you are on camera, you do the framing for them. The correct way to frame yourself in camera is to put the lens of the camera at the same level of your nose. Don't put the camera above your head and point it down or below your head and point it up. Put it on the same level.

With your camera on the same level as your nose, you frame yourself with your eyes on the eyeline in the top third of the frame, so they see you like they do in person.

Also notice that the individual's left eye is framed at the cross section of the top third of the frame and the right third. When you frame yourself in this way, you're giving the client a comfortable, interference-free, decision-making environment because it feels natural.

The helpful part of a live-online meeting is you can place your image right below your camera to see the nonverbal messages you're sending, a feature not possible in an in-person meeting. Naturally shaking your head to confirm interest and agreement can be powerful. Looking your client in the eye is much easier online as well. One of your most important nonverbal cues is a natural smile. Smiling says to your client that you like them, that you are interested in them, and that everything is OK. It creates an environment that is open, pleasant, and positive—an important influence for good in a decision-making meeting.

PLAN: EQUIPMENT

Your medium of communication in an online meeting, in addition to a computer and monitor, is the microphone, camera, and speaker. These three pieces of equipment are your eyes, ears, and airwaves carrying your client's questions, words, and image to you, and your words, questions, and image to them. Investing a little in these three things pays big dividends.

Have you ever struggled hearing your client in person? What did you do? Most likely, you got a little closer or focused more intently on what they were saying. You may have also asked them to speak up a little.

When online, if your client is soft-spoken or hard to hear, you need to be able to turn up the volume. Having an external speaker with volume control is the easiest way to solve this problem. Most likely, your laptop computer speakers are adequate at best. The best solution is an external speaker so you can quickly turn the volume up or down.

Your camera projects your presence to the client's computer, and your default laptop camera probably isn't adequate. With a quality camera, they see you without interference. The camera doesn't need to be top of the line, just one that can receive and send your picture in higher resolution. Usually 1080p will do.

PLAN: END IN MIND

Have you ever been in an online meeting that seems pointless, and you feel like you're wasting your time? Clients often feel the same way. Let's help them out. In your planning, clarify the "end in mind" for your online meeting, the decision the client needs to make. In other words, what do you want the client to say, do, or decide at the end of the meeting? An effective end in mind creates realistic and appropriate forward momentum; encourages choice, not resistance; and enables a confident decision at the end of the meeting.

PRECONDITION

Now that you have planned for the online meeting, it's time to precondition the client, which means testing the approach to the meeting and gaining the client's agreement on the end in mind and agenda (conversation checklist). It also allows you to invite the client's input, so you and the client can come prepared with clarity around priorities, pre-work, and how you'll partner together to make the online meeting a success.

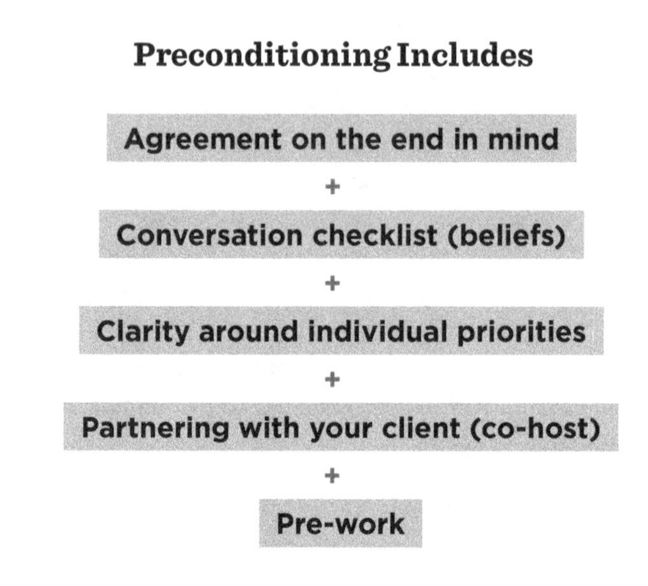

Here's a sample preconditioning email sent to a client prior to an online meeting. Notice how each preconditioning element is addressed in the fewest, most effective words.

Dear Marta,

We are looking forward to our online meeting on Friday, May 7, from 10 a.m. to 11 a.m. (GMT).

The purpose of our meeting is to find out whether or not we should continue the conversation about {product/service}. **(End in Mind)**

Based on our last meeting, to arrive at this decision, we'll need to:

- Confirm the benefits you are hoping to achieve.
- Determine quality criteria for delivery of services.
- Identify the {products/services} that meet your criteria. **(Conversation Checklist)**

Please let me know if I've missed anything. To aid our conversation, it would be helpful if you put together a list of your quality criteria for delivery of services that are most important to you. **(Priorities/Pre-work)**

You were planning on having ______ and ________ in the meeting. Did I miss anyone? Should anyone else be invited? Would you mind kicking off the meeting and introducing the agenda? **(Partnering)**

I look forward to seeing you online. The meeting link is in the invitation, but just in case, I have also included it here: Join meeting.

The platform we will be using is _____. Even if you have used that platform in the past, testing it before is helpful to avoid any "software update" delays. To test your connection, please click the following link: Test.

If you have any problems, please let me know, so we can solve any issues before our meeting. **(Pre-work)**

Let's plan to be on camera, which will allow us to communicate more effectively.

We continually get feedback that salespeople are surprised at the amount of preparation a client will put into the meeting and the appreciation they often get from clients for including an online link to test the connection. Salespeople also have reported that preconditioning has helped them avoid potential disaster when the client discovered they didn't support the online platform the salesperson was planning to use.

PRACTICE

Every professional who steps onto the stage to perform has practiced. A lot. From athletes on the field of competition, to lawyers in the courtroom, to doctoral candidates before the committee. No matter the profession, practice is paramount and the precursor to success.

When preparing for an online meeting, practice with a friend or colleague using the platform the meeting will be on. Practice sharing your screen. Practice turning screen share on and off. Remember, your client is the focus; your slides are only support. Practice asking questions and answering potential questions. Practice using names to solicit conversation. Practice being patient and persistent when unplanned events happen. Practice having people interrupt you and handling it with grace. Practice inviting people to be on camera with you. Practice, practice, practice. Consistent practice will lead to improved performance and excellent online client meetings.

INTERFERENCE

Finally, to conduct excellent online client meetings, you need to reduce interference, but not the interference you might think. It's your internal interference—the interference that prevents you from being calm when the technology takes a dive, or the dog goes berserk, or the screen share doesn't work, or you can't find the slide deck, or the document was deleted. One of the key purposes of planning, preconditioning, and practicing is to put you at ease so you can turn the volume on your internal interference way down, stay calm, and focus when things don't go perfectly.

ONLINE SUCCESS

Success in online meetings means your clients have such a wonderful experience they forget the camera, microphone, and speakers and are immersed in the conversation about the next decision they need to make to further their business.

In the past, in-person meetings were the primary way to meet with clients. Now, online meetings are the primary way to meet, and in-person meetings are secondary. Your mindset is key. An online meeting is only inferior if you think it is. It is superior when you remove interference by following the formula of plan, precondition, and practice.

We invite you to make the mental shift and do what it takes to conduct excellent online meetings. Your clients will notice, and you will stand out and sell more.

ACKNOWLEDGMENTS

We gratefully acknowledge and express our deep appreciation to the many individuals, colleagues, and clients who have helped us in our research, teaching, coaching, testing, and learning.

First, our heartfelt thanks to our amazing families for their love, sacrifice, patience, and support during the years of endless nights, weekends, and holidays while we wrote, rewrote, and strategized how to communicate these powerful principles to sales professionals around the world.

Second, thank you to Cindi Savage for her creativity, inspiration, and skills. We are deeply grateful for the hundreds of hours she spent researching, writing, rewriting, and pushing us to expand our thinking and discover what it truly means to be Strikingly Different.

Third, thanks to our clients, colleagues, associates, and team members at FranklinCovey for their feedback and help in making this book, and the entire *Strikingly Different Selling* program, a reality. We express special thanks to the following individuals:

- To our clients who generously allowed us to use their stories in this book.
- To David Marcum for his wisdom, keen insights, and undying perseverance to push on what really works. David helped us arrive at the **R+D+M=SD** formula and several other applications and examples used throughout the book and program.
- To Jeffery Downs for his passion and insights in making online meetings highly effective. Jeffery was seminal in developing the Conducting Excellent Online Client Meetings appendix in this book.
- To Meg Hackett for her incredible writing ability and experience. Meg helped us distill work sessions, coaching, and

thousands of pages of writing into practical application and an exceptional book.

- To Jody Karr, Adam Merrill, Breanne Grover, Paige Kirch, Mindy White, and the entire innovations team at FranklinCovey for their creativity and ideas that changed the way we communicate many of the examples and illustrations in *Strikingly Different Selling*.
- To Suzette Blakemore, Linda Calhoun, Susan Hall, Nicholas Harrison, Trent Merrill, Chris Roberts, Julie Schmidt, Dan Smith, Jeff Stott, and Dennis Susa for their candid and helpful feedback on early versions of the manuscript that helped us dramatically improve the book.
- To Shawn Moon, Paul Walker, and Bob Whitman for believing in us and for catching the vision of the lasting impact this work will have on the selling profession globally.

Finally, thanks to the *Strikingly Different* book team at FranklinCovey and Mango Publishing: Scott Miller, Annie Oswald, Zach Kristensen, Platte Clark, Jennifer Williams, Jodi Riedthaler, and M.J. Fièvre for their patience, thoughtful advice, and significant contributions.

ABOUT THE AUTHORS

DALE MERRILL

Dale Merrill is a global managing director in FranklinCovey's sales performance practice. He is a highly sought-after thought leader and trusted advisor to sales and business leaders at many of the world's most admired companies. Dale focuses on helping clients dramatically grow revenues and profitability.

For more than 30 years, Dale has led businesses and helped a wide range of clients solve challenges and win more business in virtually every region of the world. Prior to joining FranklinCovey, Dale served as president of a digital services company for five years, CEO of a private investment company for three years, and partner with a global technology and strategy consulting company for thirteen years. In each of his roles, he drove top-line growth by innovating new ways of thinking and executing to get different and better results.

Dale holds Bachelor of Science and Master of Accountancy degrees from the Marriott School of Management at Brigham Young University and is a Certified Public Accountant. He has advanced training in strategic management and planning (Harvard) and strategic marketing system development (Y2M). Dale loves to snow ski, wake surf, hike, mountain bike, play basketball, spikeball, and pickleball, and enjoys meeting new people all around the world. An avid reader and writer, Dale lives in the western U.S. with his family.

SCOTT SAVAGE

Scott Savage is a highly sought-after advisor, speaker, and influencer on the topics of sales, leadership, and negotiation. For more than thirty years, he has advised, coached, and trained tens of thousands of executives, consultants, and sales professionals at many of the world's largest and most successful technology, manufacturing, energy, and products companies.

Scott works regularly with sales teams across Europe, the Middle East, Asia, and the Americas. His extensive global experience is highly valued as he advises these sales leaders and their teams, who sell and negotiate in these unique marketplaces and vastly different cultures.

Scott is a global managing director in FranklinCovey's Sale Performance Practice. He holds a bachelor's degree in speech communications, and an MPA from the Marriott School of Management at Brigham Young University. In addition to authoring several articles, Scott has co-authored *The Employee Engagement Mindset* (McGraw-Hill 2012).

Scott enjoys traveling, reading, writing, hiking, running, swimming, and golf. He resides in the western Rocky Mountains of the U.S. with his wife, Cindi, and their family.

JENNIFER COLOSIMO

Jennifer Colosimo is the president of FranklinCovey's enterprise division, accountable for profitable growth globally as FranklinCovey transforms organizations by building leaders, teams, and cultures that get results in 160+ countries. Previously, she held a range of sales leadership positions at FranklinCovey in the United States, Canada, and Australia. Early in her career, she held individual contributor roles in sales and consulting, earning the company's highest awards for results and finding personal fulfillment in helping clients achieve their own great purposes.

In 2009, Jennifer co-authored the book *Great Work, Great Career* with renowned leadership expert Stephen R. Covey and has keynoted on leadership, engagement, and culture in 45 states and 12 countries.

In addition to her sales leadership roles, Jennifer has led teams in consulting, global operations, learning and development, CSR, and IT while with Andersen Consulting (now Accenture), DaVita, and FranklinCovey. Over her career, she has served as chief operations officer, chief learning officer, and vice president of wisdom.

Jennifer and her family reside in Colorado. She engages in nonprofit board service and enjoys skiing, hiking, and walking her dog Rex.

RANDY ILLIG

When it comes to sales and leadership, Randy Illig is one of the go-to professionals. An idea guy with a point of view who has an uncanny ability to also be a great listener, Randy is the global leader of FranklinCovey's Sales Performance Practice, which helps train, consult, and coach clients on how to win more profitable business. He co-authored the book *Let's Get Real or Let's Not Play: Transforming the Buyer/Seller Relationship* and is an avid reader in the sales space, constantly challenging his own ideas and those of others.

Randy consults from experience, having founded, built, and sold two successful companies: Ninety Five 5, LLC, an international sales transformation firm that served clients in the technology, management consulting, and business service sectors; and Visalign, LLC, an IT consulting firm and Microsoft Platinum Partner that served organizations in the pharmaceutical, utility, and financial sections. He's won many awards along the way including Ernst & Young's Top CEO under 40; CEO of one of Inc 500's fastest-growing companies, and the Arthur Anderson Strategic Leadership award. Most importantly, Randy is known for his sense of humor and storytelling. A native New Yorker, Randy enjoys time on the farm with his wife and daughter in upstate New York.

An alumnus of Penn State University, Randy worked in sales and sales leadership before his entrepreneurial spirit led him to go out on his own. Randy knows the day to day of chasing a quota, managing and leading sales teams, and working with clients.

INDEX

G

H

I

L

M

O

P

Q

R

S

T

V

W

About FranklinCovey

Franklin Covey Co. (NYSE: FC) is a global, public company, specializing in organizational performance improvement. We help organizations achieve results that require lasting changes in human behavior. Our world-class solutions enable greatness in individuals, teams and organizations and are accessible through the FranklinCovey All Access Pass®. They are available across multiple modalities and in 20 plus languages. Clients have included the Fortune 100, Fortune 500, thousands of small- and mid-sized businesses, numerous government entities, and educational institutions. FranklinCovey has more than 100 direct and partner offices providing professional services in more than 160 countries and territories.

READ MORE
FROM THE FRANKLINCOVEY LIBRARY

MORE THAN 50 MILLION COPIES SOLD

Learn more about how to develop yourself personally, lead your team, or transform your organization with these bestselling books, by visiting **7habitsstore.com**.

Mango Publishing, established in 2014, publishes an eclectic list of books by diverse authors—both new and established voices—on topics ranging from business, personal growth, women's empowerment, LGBTQ studies, health, and spirituality to history, popular culture, time management, decluttering, lifestyle, mental wellness, aging, and sustainable living. We were recently named 2019 *and* 2020's #1 fastest-growing independent publisher by *Publishers Weekly.* Our success is driven by our main goal, which is to publish high-quality books that will entertain readers as well as make a positive difference in their lives.

Our readers are our most important resource; we value your input, suggestions, and ideas. We'd love to hear from you—after all, we are publishing books for you!

Please stay in touch with us and follow us at:

Facebook: Mango Publishing
Twitter: @MangoPublishing
Instagram: @MangoPublishing
LinkedIn: Mango Publishing
Pinterest: Mango Publishing
Newsletter: mangopublishinggroup.com/newsletter

Join us on Mango's journey to reinvent publishing, one book at a time.

CPSIA information can be obtained
at www.ICGtesting.com
Printed in the USA
JSHW041054191221
21380JS00003B/3